THE ONLY CHILD

Literature for Life Series
General Editor: Kenyon Calthrop

The Only Child

JAMES KIRKUP

WHEATON A division of Pergamon Press

A. Wheaton & Company
A Division of Pergamon Press
Hennock Road, Exeter EX2 8RP

Pergamon Press Ltd,
Headington Hill Hall, Oxford OX3 0BW

Pergamon Press Inc.
Maxwell House, Fairview Park, Elmsford, New York 10523

Pergamon Press Canada Ltd.
Suite 104, 150 Consumers Road, Willowdale, Ontario M2J 1P9

Pergamon Press (Australia) Pty. Ltd,
P.O. Box 544, Potts Point, N.S.W. 2011

Pergamon Press GmbH,
Hammerweg 6, D-6242 Kronberg,
Federal Republic of Germany

*First published 1957 by Collins
First Published by Pergamon Press 1970
Reprinted 1974 and 1975
First published in the Literature for Life Series 1977
Reprinted 1981*

Printed in Great Britain by A. Wheaton & Co., Exeter
ISBN 0 08 006755 7

This book is dedicated to
the Kirkups, the Johnsons,
the Earls and the Falconers,
and especially to
my Mother and my Father,
with all my love

1. A Background of the Sea

THE SEA was always there, just beyond the piled-up houses and the laid-out Roman Remains. On winter nights, we could hear it roaring, pounding our broad northern beaches. In summer, on sunny holiday afternoons, we could reach it after a short, lingering walk along dazzling, tramcar-shaken Ocean Road, where the spades and pails and beach-balls and paper hats and balloons and shrimping nets and sandshoes and frilly sunshades and dolls and little yachts and celluloid windmills all rattled and whizzed and frivolled outside the postcard emporium and the sandboy toy shops, where they hung in great windy festoons of seaside fun. We would trudge along the sand-strewn pavements, past the privet-scented gates of the South Marine Park and the cat-raked rockeries of the North Marine Park, past the model of the first life-boat under its Moorish canopy, past the Wouldhave Memorial with its whey-faced clock and chinking iron cups chained to the drinking-fountain, past the Mecca Tearooms down to the pier, the Promenade, the harbour, and the wide, crowded, glittering sands. Even at the centre of the town the air had a tang of mint rock and vinegar and seaweed. Here on the beach, tracking through the grimy sand of its street-soiled approaches,

the tang was strong and heady with whiffs of laundry-like
steam from a little goods engine that chugged from time
to time along a rusty, moon-daisied track between the
sands and the working town. Sometimes it would pant
and fuss along the mile-long pier, which we were always
told was the longest in the world. Even in summer, the
green North Sea mountained and growled and crashed
along the pier's huge grey limestone blocks. Half-way
along, the dark, oil-dripping, rusty travelling crane reared
stiffly, immovably, against a vista of Tynemouth's
romantic ruined Priory, the Collingwood Memorial, the
gun-emplacements on the cliffs, and Tynemouth pier, much
shorter and duller than South Shields pier. Our lighthouse
was bigger than Tynemouth's stumpy one; it flashed a
red light at night, but Tynemouth's light was a common
white one. Our lighthouse had a tiny china doll em-
bedded in the cement between two of its great curved
blocks: if the storm gates on the pier were open, we
could walk right to the end, past the green-stepped boat
landings, and rub the china doll for luck.

From the beach, the blinding-white lighthouse appeared to rise bravely out of the shimmering, boat-netted
waves. And there, far out on the crisp horizon, the brown-
smoked tankers and trawlers trailed, crawling im-
perceptibly as the hands of the Town Hall clock down
the face of the afternoon.

*   *   *

Here, before I was born, at the mouth of the great river,
in busy, dirty, gay and happy-go-lucky South Shields—
how odd the name has always seemed to say and write!—
here my mother, a shop assistant in the Penny Bazaar,

and my father, a young man from a sea-going family, met and courted at the end of the First World War. My father had entered a solicitor's office on leaving the Board School in Ocean Road, but being an active and independent-spirited man, he soon left the office stool. Ships were his passion, and he would have liked to go to sea as his father and grandfather and great-grandfather and all our other male ancestors had done before him. But they had all been lost at sea, and when my grandmother begged my father to take a job on dry land, he renounced, to his lifelong regret, his adventurous, sea-going ambitions, and was apprenticed to a joiner. During the First World War he enlisted in the Tyneside Royal Engineers and was stationed on Inch Comb island in the Firth of Forth, where he became a sergeant-major. He married my mother, Mary Johnson, and they spent their honeymoon in Edinburgh, which my mother, who was of Scots descent, liked so much that she stayed on there until the end of the war.

When the war was over, they set up house in their home town, in a two-roomed downstairs flat in Cockburn Street, only a few doors from where my Granny Johnson lived, and here I was born.

The street was not in a good part of the town. As we say on Tyneside, it was " down street "; an American would say " on the wrong side of the tracks." I suppose it must have been a near-slum, though a respectable one on the whole. My first and most vivid memory of that house is of our front door, which was quite different from all the other front doors in the street. The paint, I remember, was new and glossy, whereas the paint on all the other front doors was a faded dull brown with round scabs where the sun had blistered it, or a shabby lightish ginger tone, improbably "grained" by the decorator. But our door was painted a smart, shiny green, and its four panels were outlined in black and gold. I don't know why our door should have been so different. I used to think it was lovely as I crawled about on our yellow-stoned doorstep on sunny days. I regarded it with joy and pride and wonder. Floating high in this shining, dark, green-and-gold heaven was our doorknob, which was of glass or brass or white china—I don't remember the colour, but the brilliance of the thing remains with me, and the distorted reflection of my own face looking up at it.

Another wonder was the boot-scraper. This was an H-shaped piece of iron let into the dark-brick wall, level with the ground, beside our front step. There was a cavity behind it, full of sandy dirt and dried mud and soot, and it seemed to me to be as black and awful as night. Nevertheless I used to put my treasures there—a blade of grass found growing inexplicably between the flagstones and the wall, a matchstick, a piece of gravel, a pink tram-ticket, a button. Occasionally a black beetle, or a wood-louse or a spider, alarmed by my baby fingers, would come scuttling out. Once I stamped on a black beetle when I had barely learned to walk, and was severely reprimanded by a group of big girls who were passing by. They told me solemnly that if you stamped on a beetle you would make it pour with rain, and now look what I had done: I had stamped on a black beetle, which was the very worst sort of beetle you could possibly stamp on, so now it would rain, it would rain cats and dogs just as they were going to the sands. I burst out crying with dismay, and they all ran off, leaving me to play with the squashed corpse at my feet.

A Background of the Sea

Early photographs show me as a pale and solemn child; from the beginning I was observant, but silent and reserved. " Wise bairn! " my Scots Granny Johnson used to say to me approvingly, when someone tried to get me to talk, and I held my tongue. It wasn't that I distrusted people; in fact, I always believed every word I was told, and took a very literal view of nursery rhymes and picturesque Tyneside expressions like " Aa'll gi' ye yor hammers," or " Haddaway hyem afore Aa gi' ye a piece o' ma tongue." I could never tell when these things were spoken in jest or in earnest, and I felt that until I knew how I was standing, it was better not to say anything. Not that, at two years of age, I hadn't a lot I wanted to say. But I kept my mouth shut and my eyes open.

At birth I was, so my mother tells me, unusually heavy and well developed. A picture taken in my first year shows me reclining on a rough green plush rug (which I loved, and still possess), and I certainly look quite a hefty baby. I have two enormous, guileless blue eyes, and an already rather uncertain smile.

I remember lying in my high pram, and the smell of that pram remains with me yet—as a little child, I must have had an extremely keen and discriminating sense of smell, for I recall the pram smell so clearly. There were the mingled aromas of warm leather and oilcloth, a faint hint of wee-wee, and the fragrance of a frilled linen pillow-slip. The pram was high and black, its interior upholstered in oilcloth patterned with tiny black and white checks. There was a sort of well at the bottom, covered by a padded lid which could be lifted out when I wanted to sit up, and kick my feet. Immense glooms descended upon me when the awkward black hood was raised, smelling of rain and damp sand, and made rigid by pressing the chromium spring fitments at the sides. I can still hear their vicious *snunk* as the hood was stretched, and the sound is followed in my memory by the rattling of heavy raindrops on its drum-tight surface.

After our front door, the next memory I have is a vague one of lying back in my pram—this, I am told, was during a summer holiday at High Force, Middleton-in-Teesdale —being wheeled by my mother and my Aunt Anna under tall, thickly-leaved trees, hearing the roaring of the Force in the distance, and cooing with delight at the bird-clattered leafy caverns overhead. Then I remember my pram running away with me in it when it had been left a moment unattended, and feeling only annoyance at leaving my mother behind, and having to be stopped by strangers. There was a feeling of dreadful impotence at not being able to tell them who I was or where I had come from. Even at that age I felt utterly exasperated by human obtuseness, and had only scorn for fatuous, baby-talk questions. I started to weep, not because I was frightened, but because these well-meaning folks all seemed so stupid, so inadequate, so completely unlike my own sensible parents. Shortly after this, I was wheeled quietly away from our front door by two little girls for whom I felt such loathing, I spat at them. When they had wheeled me back, they reported this to my mother. I felt sorry when she ticked them off for wheeling me away. And she further discomfited them by calling them " telly-pie-tits," an odd but satisfying term of infant abuse. Later I was to learn that this was the first line of a rhyme which was always being chanted at the Infants' School:

A Background of the Sea

Telly-pie-tit,
Your tongue shall be slit,
And all the little birdies
Shall have a little bit!

The horror of having one's tongue *slit* never ceased to
trouble me, and perhaps this was one of the reasons why
I was always a silent child, except when I was alone with
my mother and father.

*   *   *

I was also an only child, but not a lonely one. My
parents probably thought that the little ragamuffins in our
neighbourhood were not suitable companions for me, and
I know I was often on my own, but I didn't mind that at
all. I would be perfectly happy lying back in my pram,
looking up at the silk-fringed canopy it had on hot, sunny
days. Or I would crawl contentedly round the pavement
in front of our step, digging up the thick black dirt
between the flagstones. Or I would lie beside the boot-
scraper, looking out over the vast, steeply-cambered
stretch of cobblestones to the other side of the street.
From my pavement-level viewpoint, it was like looking
out over a high sea of stone, and discovering an unknown
land where I might never be allowed to go, where strange
children played and people who were not a bit like those
on our side of the street went about their business in queer
ways. Such washings and scrubbings of front steps and
pavements I remember from those times! Every self-
respecting housewife would " stone " her front step with
a yellow stone each morning—was it called a " Bath "
stone?—then she would wash a semi-circular piece of
pavement in front of it with a " wesh-rag " or " wesh-

cloot," the lowliest of kitchen accessories. Some fanatics would wash large areas of pavement in front of their houses, but my mother very properly thought this was carrying things too far, and I admired her for her common sense.

On summer mornings, after "the front" had been cleaned and I had had my breakfast and been washed and dressed, I was allowed to go and sit by the front door, feeling the coolness of the rapidly-drying damp pavement on my knees and hands and forearms. There I would sit and watch the big boys and girls going to school. I found them alarming, noisy and dull, but I used to wave to them, in what I think was a perfectly friendly manner. I certainly had no desire to join them, or to imitate their childish ways. They seemed such busybodies, especially the girls. One morning I was still in my pyjamas, sitting at the front door waiting for my mother to finish cleaning out and black-leading the kitchen grate. Two girls, their school satchels primly swinging, went past on the other side of the street and pretended to be immensely shocked at seeing me in my pyjamas. I felt no shame, but a very definite contempt for their sniggering silliness. I must have been about three years old when that small but illuminating incident took place. Though I was properly innocent, I was aware of the nature of evil; though my naïveté was complete, it was wide-eyed: I didn't miss a thing, and drew my own conclusions, which I kept to myself.

I had a keen ear, too, for new words and turns of phrase. Though I was always silent with strangers, I learned to talk very soon in a rapid and fluent manner with my parents, and they may have warned me not to repeat certain bad words which I heard in the street. Occasionally,

I remember, I would go to my mother and whisper in her ear that I had just heard someone say something bad.

" What was it?" she would ask, smiling.

" I don't like to say it," I would reply. " It was bugger."

What a chill of horror used to run through me as I said the awful word! My mother would pretend to be terribly shocked.

" He shouldn't have said that, should he?" she would say gravely.

" No, he shouldn't have said bugger," I would reply, with pious relish.

Then we would laugh together over the man's wicked stupidity, and I would promise never to use " that word " myself. It was a happy and sane way of sending the Devil packing.

About this time too, some little girls teased me by saying that they would tell my mother I had been using bad language to them. I was overwhelmed by the monstrousness of the lie; I was too simple to see that it was all just a rather nasty piece of bluff. Miserably frightened, I felt I could never face my mother and father again, and decided to " run away." I did not get much farther than the corner of our back lane, where I hung about in the gathering darkness for what seemed to me to be hours. I watched the lamplighter with the spark burning at the end of his long pole light all the gas-lamps in Robertson Street. The men came tramping home from work, and I kept out of my father's sight when I saw him coming. I was sick at heart, and cold, and hungry. It was autumn, the long nights were coming on, and the ships moving down the river to the open sea blew lingering, melancholy blasts on their sirens, and the fog-horn began to hoot. Eventually I went home, shaking with cold and misery, and was met on our front doorstep by my bewildered mother, to whom I told my tearful tale, passionately protesting my innocence. I still remember the pang of joy I felt when I realised that the girls had *not* told her lies about me, and the wonderful feeling of security and self-confidence I had when she said:

" We know you wouldn't say *that* sort of thing, hinney! "

How my heart ached with love for her, who loved me so much, so perfectly, and who understood my innocence! My father, too, helped to drive away my awful fear with a great burst of laughter. I was hoisted on to the kitchen table, where the bobbled tablecloth had been drawn back, and my hands and face and finally my knees were washed in warm, soap-clouded, carbolic-scented water. It was grand to see one knee washed clean and rosy, and the other beside it, still black with grime. Then supper, and nursery rhymes on my father's lap, and several performances of *This little piggy went to market*, played on my firelit toes; then off to bed in the " front room " which was also my parents' bedroom. There the gas lamp in the street outside would be casting its pale, lemon-yellow moonlight through the stiff white lace window-curtains on to the plaster-decorated ceiling. And as I lay there, warm and happy, watching the slightly-stirring shadows of the flowery lace, and listening to the far-off moaning of the ships, I would drift off into long, deep sleep, a sleep without fear, without care, lulled by the gentle breathing of the sea beyond the pitheads and the houses.

2. *Friends and Relations*

I GOT past the toddling stage and began to extend my field of knowledge. But though I was " growing out of " the pram and though my interest in the boot-scraper and the front step was not so concentrated, my life was still very much bounded by our street. Now I ventured to cross it in order to reach the " shop end," which was only three or four doors away; sometimes I would even make an expedition to the other end, the distant " cemetery end," which must have been over twenty doors away from ours.

Cockburn Street was almost a cul-de-sac, for at the end farthest from our house there was what seemed to me to be an insurmountably high wall. A little back lane ran between the wall and the last houses, and behind the wall lay a churchyard full of tilted gravestones, grimy marble urns, statues of angels and veiled women, and slanting stone tables off which the dead were supposed to eat their suppers after dark.

I shall never forget the first time I was " bunked up " —that is, given a leg-up—on to the top of the wall. Except for when my father had held me up high with my top-not curls touching the warm, dust-smelling, white-washed infinity of our kitchen ceiling, I had never been so high before. I was frightened and enthralled by the dizzy height as I sat astride the wall which, I seem to remember, from a tingling of scraped knees and palms, was covered with rough concrete. Maybe there was broken glass up there too. When I forgot to be frightened, I looked out, with a swimming sensation in my head, over a sea of leaning gravestones. It was a curious sea. I was quite used to the *real* sea—there was never anything unusual about that. But this was an inland one, half-motionless, half-moving: for between the graves long grasses waved and tottered among the jam jars holding dead wallflowers and marguerites. In the distance was a church, I believe, black and sooty, with a yellowed clock staring across at me. Beyond that, the faint sounds of the docks rose with clouds of brown and grey and white smoke from the shipyards and the river.

I think I must have been " bunked up " on to the wall by some children from another street; I can't remember them at all. But while I was stuck up on top of the wall, they told me fearful tales of ghosts rising from under their stone tables and tramping up and down our street and making terrible munching noises as they ate their cold meat pies and pease pudding and pigs' trotters and chips on their filthy grave-tables, among the long, sooty grasses. I began to scream with terror, and they ran away, leaving me perched helplessly on the wall. I don't know what I would have done if just at that moment a kindly pitman had not passed by on his way home from the morning shift. He was black all over, but when he held his arms out to me I gladly let myself fall into them: his blackness was better than the ghastly whiteness of the dead. As soon as I had my feet on the ground again—how weak my knees felt!—I ran home and told my mother everything I had seen and heard. Not even all her tender re-assurances could quite drive the pictures of the dead out of my mind. I had not yet seen a dead person, and I doubt if I could have been told what death meant, but as soon as I heard about those ghosts, I seemed to recognise them, like long-lost friends. I knew what they were, and though I felt instinctively that they would not want to harm me, a fear—a human, earthly fear—had been put into my mind, and I could not get rid of it. Ever after that, the stirring of the lace curtains over the window at dusk, the crunching sound of miners' hobnailed boots as they came back from the nightshift, the voice of the " knocker-up " at five in the morning and the gloomy hooting of the tankers and cargo-ships moving out into the vast unknown of the North Sea became the movements and the voices of the ghosts themselves. Before I learned to recognise the sound of my own heart beating, I would lie awake in the darkness listening to the pulse of blood in my head, and think it was the tramping of ghostly feet. And once, early in the morning, lying in my bed and listening to my parents talking in the kitchen, I heard a voice just beside me saying: " Jimmy! " It only spoke once, but I knew it was not a human voice. It was a ghost's voice. My heart beat faster, but with expectancy, not fear. I felt that I wouldn't mind being talked to by a ghost. But it did not speak again, and I fell asleep.

*   *   *

Curiously enough, I can remember nothing of the little shop at the corner of the street. Shops are supposed to fascinate children; certainly I was not fascinated. There was a smell of dog biscuits and blue-mottled soap, and that was all. It was obviously a very poor sort of establishment. I remember rather better the off-licence which was either in or near our street. The smell of beer always seemed so totally unpleasant, I could not imagine why my Granny Johnson used to drink the horrid stuff.

My maternal grandmother was a native of Berwick-on-Tweed. Her maiden name was Margaret Borthwick, and her father owned the Berwick Arms, which was a large and prosperous public house. My Granny used to serve in the bar when she was a girl. It was a big house, with a billiards room. Mr. Borthwick had salmon-fishing rights on the Tweed, and a fleet of fishing-boats too. He was very sensitive about his name. It was said that a Borthwick had once betrayed and sold his king, and he never liked to be reminded of the fact. At election times, when everyone in Berwick went and stood on the steps of the Town Hall and proclaimed whom they were voting for, my great-grandfather would announce to the public who came to throw rotten eggs at men who did not vote for the candidate in favour that *he* never took a bribe, although he *was* a Borthwick, and that was more than most of those assembled there could say.

My Granny married an Irishman of good family from Balla in County Mayo. His father had married a Mary Kenavan, after whom my mother is named. But she died, and old Mr. Johnson married a second time. My grandfather, not liking his stepmother, ran away from home at the age of fourteen, and never went back, though in later years he admitted that he had been in the wrong. He used to say: " The best fools come from Ireland, but the biggest fools go there." Though his family were well-to-do, he had to walk five miles to school. He was a quiet, gentle man, and my mother always said I " took after " him.

Friends and Relations

When I think of my Granny Johnson now, I see a commanding, imperial figure, always dressed in black, wearing a tidy black alpaca apron. She was always sitting down; she had a fine head and a straight back, and she sat on her little kitchen chair as if it were a throne. I retain an impression of jet brooches, ear-rings, beads. Her hair must have been white, but I do not remember it so. I seem to remember it as snuff-coloured, but perhaps this is an association of ideas with the snuff she was in the habit of taking, very discreetly. Her nostrils, I noticed, were always slightly brown; and when she pressed me to her stiff black dress, I could smell snuff and a hint of stout, and the warm, sweet fragrance of silk. " Oh! ma knees! " she used to exclaim, in a mock music-hall manner. She had a strong Scots accent, which I quickly learned to imitate. But though she " thought the world of me," and spoilt me quite outrageously, I would never have dared to mimic her accent in her presence. I loved her dearly, but mingled with that love was a kind of awe: she seemed so terribly old, and I had to respect someone so impressively ancient.

Though she was old, she still seemed to rule her household with a kindly firmness. Her eyes were mild but penetrating, and she was capable of a dry and caustic wit, that has descended, though in a gentler form, to my mother. She had had a tough life. At one time she had run a fish-and-chip business in Berwick, but it had failed because, as my mother said, she had " too good a heart " and no business sense. She had had many children: one of them, my Uncle Charles, whom I never knew, but whose lively and gifted children were to be a great delight to me later on, had been killed in the Great War. Another of her sons was a schoolmaster in Berwick, and yet

The Only Child

another, Uncle Jack, had gone even farther away—to Bermuda, where he worked in a hotel in Hamilton. But he used to write to us, and letters from Bermuda were a great excitement. He once sent us a bottle of fine, pink sand from the beaches of Bermuda, so that we could compare it with our own coarse brown stuff, which I was sure was better for making " pot-pies " (sand-pies) with.

But Granny Johnson still had some of her children around her, and they were devoted to her. There was my bachelor Uncle Bob, who had been gassed in the Somme, and bore the marks of it on his broad, good-natured face. I was always a little scared of his loud voice, but I liked his merry laugh and roguish eyes and the accuracy of his aim when he spat in the grate. When he washed and shaved, he would tuck a towel in the neckband of his Union shirt, and let it hang down his back, which I thought was most unusual, because my father didn't do it that way at all, but draped the towel round the front as well as the back. It was always interesting, but puzzling, and even a little disturbing, to see things done in what I considered to be the wrong way, for I believed my parents' ways were the only right ones. But I used to like to sit and watch my Uncle Bob shaving his fierce red face, with his braces dangling, and the towel hanging right down his back.

In the same Cockburn Street house too, lived my Aunt Lyallie. It was an odd name, but a pretty one, with its echoes of lilac and lily: it was a name peculiar to our family, but I never found out what its origin was. Aunt Lyallie, too, had a charming Scots accent: she had lived some years in Berwick and Burnmouth and Eyemouth, where some of our relatives were fisherfolk. Like my grandmother, she was caustic and dry-spoken, yet gay and

24

delightfully girlish, much more uninhibited than my mother, but with all her steady warmth of heart. She had a little black Pomeranian dog called Rosie who was a most affectionate animal; she would run to welcome me whenever I climbed my Granny's steep, canvas-covered back stairs, and would jump on to my lap when I sat down, and lick my face with her rough little pink tongue.

" Puir little beastie! " my Granny would say to her, as she supped a saucer of tea. Rosie was sometimes teased by my Aunt Lyallie's three strapping sons, whom I adored for their dashing sense of fun, their animal spirits, their " gift of the gab," and their adventurous lives. Two of them were in the Coldstream Guards, and had been to India. The youngest, whom I think I liked best of all, had a marvellous, full-hearted laugh.

" If only I could laugh like that! " I used to think. But I never could. This cousin was an excitable, animated, sensitive young man who played the fiddle very well. I used to like to sit on the " clippy " mat in front of my Granny Johnson's kitchen fire and listen to him practising scales and playing *The Minstrel Boy*, or *We'll Reel the Keel Row*. He and my mother, who was a sweet singer, were the first to awaken my passion for music and dancing. I would sit quietly waiting in my Granny's house, hoping, if he was out, that he would come in soon and play his fiddle. I would sit watching him shave and brushing his teeth: that in itself was a marvel, for he would put his toothbrush up the chimney and brush his teeth with soot. They were the whitest teeth I've ever seen. Then he would light a Woodbine and spend a long time polishing his shoes and combing his hair: that house always smelt of shaving-soap, and shoe-polish, and hair-oil and cigarettes. Then, after a cup of tea—there was always a

pot of tea being " mashed " at my Granny Johnson's—
he would say, while I listened with bated breath:

" Well, I think I'll have a bit scrape at the old fiddle."

And I would sit trembling with expectancy while he
opened the violin-case, took out his fiddle and rosined his
bow. The inside of the violin-case was beautiful and
strange. It was lined with royal-blue velvet, and there
were two little boxes inside, where the waist of the violin
came, full of pegs and bits of rosin. There was a larger
box at the narrow end, in which he kept a tangle of
" Cathedral " strings. And how elegant was the rosewood bow, inlaid with ivory and mother-of-pearl! Then
he would set up his little, rickety gilt music-stand, and
draw his bow across the strings, producing chords that
sent shivers down my back, after which he would begin
practising his scales and exercises while I looked on spellbound, listening to every note, watching his left-hand
crab up and down the strings, and his right hand rising
and falling and suddenly plucking a thrilling *pizzicato*.
It was all enchantment, and I looked upon him as a
magician, his handsome, pointed face cradled on the chin-
rest, and a long lock of dark hair falling over his brow.
Then from time to time he would look at me and give
me a prodigious wink, and smile dazzlingly and go on
playing; I thought this was the cleverest thing of all, to
be able to play, and wink at the same time. He played for
a while in a picture palace with a pianist who accompanied
the last of the silent moving pictures. Later on, when I
read about Paganini, I would think of my cousin Tom—
thin, volatile, tall and wild—and remember his clever
hands, his grin, and his devilish wink.

There was another member of the household, an Uncle
Martin, whom I remembered only vaguely as someone

gentle, pale, and rather strange, with a drooping moustache and a quiet manner that I found very reassuring among the hurly-burly of my Granny's house. He used to take me for walks. I remember toddling along beside him, holding his hand, and being told that we were "going to the Library." This was the Public Library in Ocean Road, where, after looking longingly at the model of a three-master in its glass case, I would be dragged away to the News Room. Here there were always down-and-outs, seafaring men without a ship, unemployed miners wearing white mufflers, and caps set very straight on their heads, all reading the morning papers and last night's *South Shields Gazette and Shipping Telegraph*. It was a mournful place, especially on a damp day. We were not allowed to speak. The newspapers were on racks, well above my head. I used to stand patiently and quietly beside my Uncle Martin while he read the day's news, peering at the print through steel-rimmed glasses. All I could see were the boots and trouser-legs of the men reading the papers on the other side of the rack. I got to know some of those boots and trousers quite well. The boots were generally old army boots, damp and wrinkled and patched, with sodden bootlaces. I knew the miners because they had metal-capped boots. Sometimes there would be a pair of seaman's boots, with thick blue woollen stockings turned down over the tops. Most were battered, down-at-heel; some had obviously had a great deal of care spent on them, and though clumsily cobbled their old leather tops shone with spit and polish. There were also pathetic pairs of worn-out, brown sandshoes with flapping crêpe soles, their uppers full of holes: sometimes a dirty big toe could be seen working, its grey nail long and dead.

27

The Only Child

The trousers were of all kinds, too—blue denims, greasy and frayed; patched dungarees, with idle foot-rules in the long, narrow side pocket—" my rule pocket," as father called it; oily moleskins, white house-painters' trousers with the bottoms of another pair showing underneath; cast-off postmen's and policemen's trousers; shiny blue serge trousers; muddy roadmen's whipcord trousers, old baggy tweeds and fold-marked bell-bottoms. Seen from this point of view, there was something infinitely pathetic about them; and though I was not conscious of this at the time, Shakespeare's view of man as a " poor forked creature " was one that I had discovered for myself at the age of four or so.

My Uncle Martin's trousers seemed to me to be quite extraordinary. I remember distinctly setting off with him one day from the corner of Cockburn Street. We were " going to the Library." I was walking on his left, my right hand clasped in his left hand. He was wearing golden, beer-coloured corduroy trousers. I thought they were very odd, but beautiful. And those trousers are what I remember best about my Uncle Martin. I always sensed that he was a little odd himself, and so I did not mind the oddness of his trousers. They were the sort of things he would naturally wear, and so everything was all right. I always had an acute sense of what was " right " and " fitting," and any departure from my rigid conventional standards I found most distressing.

At the age of four I was not consciously aware of all these things, but I can still remember being very sensitive to atmospheres and occasions, and being disturbed and unsatisfied without knowing why. At my Granny Johnson's, however, I was vividly aware of her household's inextinguishable zest for life, and felt sharply the vitality and the charm of those people who could sing and laugh and play and talk the hind leg off a donkey—they were all so different from myself. I was often puzzled, wondering why I couldn't be like them.

I suffered, it seemed, from a terrible handicap—the inability to make a noise. I noticed that other people and other children could enter a room or a shop in a way that made you realise at once that they were there. But other people, adults and children, who always seemed to be surrounded and as it were partially deafened by the busy hum of their own bodies always took a long time to become aware of my presence; when they did, I often seemed to give them an unpleasant shock.

" You gave me a nasty turn! " the fat, pinafored old lady who kept the corner shop would say accusingly, reproachfully, subsiding into her endlessly twittering cane chair and breathing hard with the shock of seeing my head just below her counter, where I would stand, motionless and silent, waiting to be attended to while she stooped and gasped over her sweeping and tidying behind her towers of blue-mottled soap.

I just didn't know how to shout, or even how to talk fairly loudly: my feet never made a sound, and my whole body felt light and still. This inability to make a noise embarrassed me, and people's reactions—usually violent and cross—to my silent comings and goings disturbed me, made me blush till I thought my head would burst. I would try to make some kind of natural commotion as I entered a room or the corner shop, but the noises I made were never bold enough: they were still beyond the reach of human ears. Only the cats could hear me coming.

" By gum, I thowt you were a ghost! " people would cry, to my acute distress, when they suddenly found me standing beside them in the street or at a doorway. I often began to feel as if I had indeed materialised out of nothing, out of thin air, and that I didn't altogether belong to this world where my feet made no sound on the ground as other children's did, and where it was so important to be able to make a noise. Only my mother and father were always immediately aware of my presence, though my behaviour with them was usually no less silent than with strangers.

However hard I tried to make a noise, I always remained silent and faintly troubled. My grandmother's household looked upon my silences, my inarticulate agitations and my dumb happiness with tolerant amusement. I had no thoughts of whether they loved me or whether I loved them: it was enough to be allowed occasionally to be in their presence, to be a witness of their animal spirits and their gaiety. It was at that early age that the pattern of my life and personality began to appear. I was a lonely child, though I was not conscious of loneliness; in fact, I preferred being on my own. At the same time I was torn by the desire to be with people, to be part of a circle; I loved the idea of " being together " with Whitmanesque intensity. Yet after " being together " with my cousins for a while, I longed to be alone. I couldn't understand myself. It was the beginning of a conflict that was to distress me for many years.

*   *   *

In spite of their brave gaiety, my cousins had a hard life. There wasn't much work for anyone, especially for Tom, who was a blacksmith to trade. Money was always short, and Aunt Lyallie " went out to work." I remember being taken by my mother to a seamen's hotel near the river where my aunt was working in the kitchen. It was a grim place. There was an enormous kitchen table of scrubbed deal boards, and the chairs were old and hard. The gas was on all the time: it must have been a basement. The cook, a big, red-haired woman wearing a man's cap with several ornamental hat-pins skewered into it, made us a cup of tea in a huge, chipped, blue enamel teapot; she had to use both hands to lift it. I had to put up with a good deal of the usual chaff and banter—what had I done with my tongue?—had the cat got it?—I should have been a little girl, and all that—all perfectly kindly and good natured, but I found it acutely distasteful. I blushed very easily. Whenever someone spoke to me, I could feel the dreadful heat rising to my head, suffusing my face and making my ears tingle and my eyes water. I can still see the cook, in her man's cap, wearing a sack as an apron, roaring with laughter against a background of grey boilers and black ranges and a sad, barred window, making strong tea and cutting " doorsteps "—thick slabs of dry bread—which she covered liberally with golden syrup. One of the most colourful of my early memories is of the five-pound tin of Tate and Lyle's Golden Syrup standing like a green-and-golden set-piece in the centre of that vast kitchen table and shining like a good deed in a naughty world. The ornate lettering and the picture of the lion and the bees with the motto: " Out of strength came forth sweetness " were pictorial and literary puzzles that I longed to solve. The cook ladled the syrup lavishly with a long-handled wooden spoon on to the hunks of un-buttered bread. I can still recall the odd taste of the missing butter—if I may coin an Irishism. I thought it was not right at all.

Also on the table was an outsize tin of Nestlé's Condensed Milk (Sweetened). We used this at home in our
tea, though *our* tin was much smaller: we pierced a
couple of holes in the top, and let the thick, sticky milk
trickle in an amusing spiral into the hot black tea; it left
ghostly trails on the surface before you stirred it up. I
liked the picture of the nest on this tin, and the festoons
of medals won at long-past international exhibitions. The
words " Fit for Babies " were among the first I learned
to read. My father disliked and distrusted anything
tinned: " condemned milk " he used to call it. When I
started school and learned to read fluently, I would spend
all teatime reading the close-set print on the Nestlé's tin;
the instructions for feeding babies I found particularly
enjoyable. Another source of early reading matter was
the H.P. Sauce bottle, and the bottle of " Camp " Coffee
Extract that they used at my Granny Johnson's, with its
gorgeous Eastern label and its instructions which included,
I believe, the warning: " Don't be misled! " I used to
pronounce this last word as " mizzled," to the great
amusement of my Aunt and cousins. They used condensed milk, too, but it was skimmed milk, which my
father disapproved of. The tin had a vivid green picture
of Ireland the Emerald Isle and colleens and cows on it.
" Green denotes poison," my father would say, and so I
would never drink tea with skimmed milk in it. " Oh,
divvent be sae parky, man! " my Uncle Bob would growl.
But my father's word was law. I would refuse to drink
the tea; blushing furiously, but not saying a word, I
would sit looking at the violent green label, and at their
faces, expecting them all to drop dead, as they supped the
tainted tea from their pretty flowered saucers. Rosie the
Pomeranian had a saucerful, too; she lapped it up daintily,

never spilling a drop. None of them ever did drop dead, and I don't think I ever really expected them to, for they were special people, protected by their own magic.

*　　　*　　　*

Another Cockburn Street character whom I remember very well was Mrs. Battey, our upstairs neighbour. In a crowded street of small houses, and especially in a long row of " up and downs " like ours, it was most important, for those living on the ground floor, to have a good upstairs neighbour, and good neighbours on each side. A good upstairs neighbour was one who didn't stamp about and shake off the downstairs gas mantles; one who used the stairs as quietly as possible, and didn't slam the front door. A good neighbour also meant someone who would come in and help when the new wallpaper was being put up, when there was illness or trouble in the house, when there was childbirth or death, when a " clippy " rug was being made and when there was a removal to a new house. A bad neighbour banged on the walls if you made the slightest noise: if you lived upstairs, he would bang on the ceiling with a broom-shank; he would be noisy and dirty and use bad language and not sweep his part of the front street.

But Mrs. Battey was " a canny body," a good neighbour and a generous friend. She was a very large, florid, good-tempered, excitable lady; she was almost stone-deaf, and had the very penetrating voice the deaf often have. She screamed like a gaudy cockatoo when she laughed. She looked like one at times, as she waddled round our little backyard. She had a beaky nose and pince-nez—gold-rimmed glasses of which she was very proud; they shook and flashed when she let off her screams of laughter. Whenever she " held forth," she showered her listeners with " spit." She had the first set of false teeth I ever saw, with bright orange gums. They were possibly too big for her: they protruded, and gave her smiles a brilliant, lopsided look; they kept dropping and slipping and clicking unexpectedly, in a manner which as a little boy I found interesting. She had a small, silent husband who worked on the railway, and whom she always addressed in full: " Mister Battey! " she would shout to him out of the upstairs window, or: " Thomas Battey, I want you up here! " And poor Mr. Battey, a burnt-out Woodbine hanging on his lower lip, would trudge up and down the back stairs with pails of coal or buckets of water. I don't recollect anything more about her husband, except that he used to scrub the backyard in his bare feet with an enormous " Corporation " street-broom. But Mrs. Battey provides me with one of my most alarming childhood memories.

When she had shopping to do down in the town, my mother would occasionally leave me with Mrs. Battey. I would sit upstairs in her kitchen while she scrubbed or baked a batch of loaves, listening to her endless stream of chatter. Generally speaking, people with loud voices and high laughs used to terrify me—my exuberant male cousins were rather upsetting in this respect—but I was quite happy with Mrs. Battey, although I never knew what she was going to say or do next.

There were so many new things to look at in her kitchen. She had a bed that folded up into a mahogany cupboard. Did she call it a " dess bed," or did I not hear aright? Her " clippy " mats had a different texture from ours; they had weird, straggling patterns on them, and she wasn't as fond as my mother of " mixy-maxy "

34

centres. Her tablecloth was of wine-coloured velours, with a deep, tasselled fringe round the edge, whereas ours was a faded pink cotton one, edged with strawberry-shaped bobbles. I remember sitting on my little chamber-pot—how cold the china rim was when you first sat down!—and playing with those soft, dangling bobbles while I " did my duty." They were not attached very firmly, and after playing with one for a while I would find it coming away in my hand, like a little ripe fruit. There were a lot of bobbles missing from our tablecloth.

The patterns on her wallpaper and canvas floor-covering were extraordinarily different from ours; I thought they were too strange and hideous for words, but I never said so. The wallpaper in Mrs. Battey's kitchen had a brownish background covered with a pattern of dull red and eggy-yellow leaves and pale fawn flowers which Mrs. Battey proudly identified as " Dusty Millers." The canvas on the floor had a dizzy pattern of green lilies and purple grapes on imitation brown tiles with an orange-squiggled border. It was an interlocking pattern, and my eyes would become dazed and weary as I tried obsessively to understand its tortured, meaningless logic.

It was always stiflingly hot in her little kitchen, for she liked to keep a good fire going even in the height of summer. Her fire-irons, brass fender and black-leaded " fire tidy " round the ash-pan were clean and shining, just like my mother's downstairs. She, too, whitewashed her hearth afresh every morning, after raking out the ash-pit and the flues. The oven door of her kitchen range was exactly the same as ours, but the design of the little ventilator-windows that slid open or shut at the top was not quite the same as ours. I liked opening and shutting those tiny windows, even when the little knob on the shutter was almost too hot to touch; and sometimes I got into trouble for opening them when my mother had a batch of scones baking in the oven. I didn't dare touch Mrs. Battey's oven-ventilator: I was sure it would be too hot to hold; the heat of her enormous fire made the oven tick and rattle alarmingly, and whenever she opened the oven door she used an " oven-cloth." How she *clashed* the door!

Another unusual but reassuring sight was Mrs. Battey's gas mantle. Its moon-like whiteness was unmarred by any hole or tear. In our street, the " mantle " was almost a sacred object. Ours was always a centre of anguished worry to me since the day when, dancing on the kitchen table, I had touched it with my finger and found it suddenly crumbled away into a fine white dust. Then we had to get a new one, which we could ill afford. How carefully we carried it home in its cardboard carton! When my father had fixed it on the jet and lit it, it flared up alarmingly, and for a time gave no light at all: it was all horribly sooty, and the burning gas inside twinkled desperately inside its little black bag, winking through thousands of tiny holes. Then it slowly turned a deep red, then bright orange, then yellow, then burned to a pure, incandescent whiteness. Whenever I think of Purity, I can't help remembering our gas mantle burning with that hard, fierce light. We would look up at it anxiously to see if it wobbled when the Batteys were moving about— sometimes rather heavily—upstairs. How fragile it looked! How much more fragile than an egg-shell! It was more like a flake of snow against the dingy whiteness of the ceiling: it was like the moon seen in daylight.

We used what I believe is called an " inverted " mantle, which hung down. Mrs. Battey, I noted with interest, used the more expensive and larger "incandescent" mantle, which stood upright on its gas-bracket, inside a lamp-shade of fluted pink glass. It made an ominous hissing sound when lit, but I was relieved to see that it was without the slightest fracture. It was a perfect, snowy cone, and its unimpaired purity made me feel at ease, happy and secure. But the feeling of being "upstairs" and looking out dizzily through the ocre-rinsed lace curtains over the brick walls and slate roofs of the back streets was one I did not care for. It made my inside creep: it was "not right," I thought, to be so far removed from the ground, and I suffered from an illusion of perpetual falling.

But one afternoon my sense of propriety was rudely shattered. I had been left in Mrs. Battey's kind and capable charge. I was sitting quietly on her cracket, trying to avoid looking at the window and keeping out of range of the "spit." Three of her friends came in— jolly, bosomy and forthright South Shields matrons. I had the feeling that Mrs. Battey looked upon them as somewhat lower than herself in the social scale, but how I received this impression I do not know. In those days, I could feel a great deal more than I could understand. Perhaps they were rather less well dressed than she was: at least one of them had a black woollen shawl over her head, which was something Mrs. Battey would never have descended to—she went in for smart hats piled with fruit and nodding feathers and clumps of artificial roses.

The three friends had been to a sale of cloth remnants —a weekly event called "Remnant Day" which was held at Crofton's, a large store in the Market Place. Perhaps that was where my mother had been: my father, with his love of word-play and broad sense of fun, nicknamed it

37

" Rag-rent Day." These three women brought back some of the excitement and uproar of Crofton's on Rag-rent Day with them, as they triumphantly shouted details of the bargains they had found. Their chatter seemed to nonplus Mrs. Battey for a while: her own garrulous flow was dammed, and she had the greatest difficulty to get a word in. All she could say was an occasional: " Gan*non*, hinney! " " Nivver in the world! " (pronounced " whorled "), and " Haddaway, wummon! " when one of her friends, with formal politeness, protested that they wouldn't dream of troubling her to make tea for them. That was Mrs. Battey's cue. She banged her big black kettle on the roaring fire and got out her best willow-pattern cups and saucers and her cut-glass milk jug. Then she started talking at the top of her voice about the bargains *she* had found in her time. She screamed and crowed, and as always when she was excited, foam appeared at the corners of her mouth and she spat more copiously than ever. Her head wagged, her arms were stretched wide as an angler's, her spectacles joggled and flashed, and her heavy, homely body stumped round the kitchen as she made the tea.

Then the awful thing happened. Stung, perhaps, to jealousy by her friends' triumphs, she bent down, lifted up her voluminous skirts and proudly displayed her new knickers to her admiring friends. She had on a pair of great, baggy beige bloomers which she claimed she had made for eleven pence out of a remnant bought on Remnant Day. Her friends felt the material and tested the strength of the elastic. Mrs. Battey was, after all, giving them tea, so they uttered flattering coos and exclamations as Mrs. Battey kept turning round and round, basking in their admiration, with her skirt well up.

Friends and Relations

I was, I suppose, a very prim little boy, though no more of a prig than most children, who have generally a very acute sense of what is fitting, and disapprove of anything that breaks accepted rules or offends against conventional standards of propriety. Mrs. Battey's exposure of her bloomers seemed to me then an unpardonable outrage, an insult to my dignity; and though I remained sitting sedately in my chair, I longed to get up and run away. I felt myself blushing furiously, and wanting to weep with shame and embarrassment.

Perhaps I had been influenced by the little girls in our street, who sometimes wore knickers and more often didn't. They used to talk with a kind of excited prudery about their knickers: there was always a great deal of whispering about who wore knickers and who didn't. It was shameful, according to them, for one's knickers to be seen, and simply scandalous if they were to come down below the hem of one's frock: they always seemed to be hauling them up under their dresses, with a great show of primness. Yet these same girls used to tuck their frocks quite openly into the tops of their knickers when they went " plodging " at the seaside, or when they did hand stands or " the crab " or cart wheels, or when they played those interminable ball-games in which the ball has to be bounced on the pavement and through the straddled legs to hit the wall behind. Did they call them " One Ball " and " Two Ball? " I remember that one of the rhymes they chanted as they played these games began:

> One allairy,
> Two allairy,
> One two three!

The Only Child

Four allairy,
Five allairy,
In the sea!

Such games were a mystery to me. I was never any good at them myself, for I sometimes tried them out when no one was looking. The rules were highly complicated and varied almost from street to street. There were often heated arguments between blue-bloomered gangs of girls about how often the ball had to be bounced before the leg was cocked over it, whether it was the right leg or the left leg that had to be cocked, how high up the wall the ball should be allowed to bounce, and so on. I was bothered and disgusted by their bulging knickers. What really excited me was the chant that accompanied the bouncing, a queer, sing-song chanting that had something rather suggestive about it. I remember one which went:

Heel, toe,
Allairy, O!
Ower the watter
She must go!
Heel, toe,
Allairy, O!
What's the matter
Wi' Auntie Flo!

Another went:

Each, peach, pear, plum,
Out goes Tom Thumb.
Tom Thumb is in the wood,
I spy Robin Hood.
Robin Hood is in the cellar,
I spy Cinderella.

There was another very popular one which indicated the appropriate actions there were to be performed while the ball was bouncing:

> Plainsey, clapsey,
> Tour the world to backsey,
> Touch your knee,
> Touch your toe,
> Touch your shoulder
> And under you go,
> Heel, toe, allairy, O!

Another ball-bouncing rhyme was:

> Ower the garden waall,
> I let the baby faall;
> Me mother came oot
> An' give me a cloot,
> She ast us whatt it wuz aal aboot,
> She said she'd torn us inside oot,
> Ower the garden waall.

The only other one I can remember completely is:

> Ipsy, gipsy,
> Lived in a tent,
> She couldn't afford
> To pay the rent.
> The rent man came
> The very next day,
> The gipsy ran away,
> Ower the hills and far away.

But let us return to Mrs. Battey's kitchen. After she had had my painful blushes pointed out to her by her three friends, she dropped her skirt, and shouted:

" Ee, hinneys, what a gan-on! "

They uttered great peals of jovial laughter, and beamed at me for being such an " owld-fashioned bairn." Their faces were flushed with success and hot tea. They gave me a cake, which I could not eat for misery. I felt the whole civilised world had tumbled down about my stinging ears. Eventually my mother came home and I was able to creep down the back stairs and tell her all about it, with many tears. She understood my shame at once, and yet managed to make it look funny, as always when I became too intense about anything. That gentle mockery, that kindly common-sense were often brought into skilful play to alleviate the many curious and inexplicable agonies I suffered. One of the most useful characteristics I have inherited from her is the capacity to laugh at myself. This is not always an enviable gift. If one does not appear to take oneself seriously, other people often refuse to do so. People who are " solemn-sides " cannot account for self-mockery, so it has its uses, for it keeps the fools at bay, though intensity and exaggeration, to which I am rather prone, are not despicable qualities either. My mother helped me to see the need to keep a balance between my emotions and my intellect in an effective and sensible way; all the more effective, perhaps, because of its gay, unassuming wisdom, its unconscious sense of order and proportion.

From this early period of my childhood, I can remember very little about my parents except that they loved me and I loved them—though I did not think of it as " love." The word had no significance for me then, and if anyone had asked me: " Do you love me? " I should have had to say: " What do you mean? " My parents were simply large, kind, beautiful people with whom I felt happy and safe: I did not see them as individuals until several years later, and I did not adore one more than the other as I believe some children do. Up to the time I started school I was with them constantly, and I never tired of their company. I remember the happiness of lying on my mother's lap—the warmth of her arms, the sweet, homely smell of a freshly-laundered cotton " pinny," and the miraculous softness of her smiling face, that I loved to stroke. I remember, too, the bliss of sitting on my father's knee as he read to me or talked to me; I would lean back contentedly against his waistcoat or the bib of his dungarees and smell the delightful aroma of pipe tobacco and wood shavings that always hung around him. The fire in the high, black-leaded grate would glow and click over the whitewashed hearth; I would feel his military moustache against my cheek, giving me a sudden, ticklish kiss that made my spine shiver with pleasure. No one could ever have had such wonderful parents.

3. My Father's Side

Apart from a certain little friend whom I must give a whole chapter to later on, I remember no one else from Cockburn Street with any sort of clarity. But I have faint memories of two strange children and their mother—a dark-haired, slant-eyed boy and girl, delicate and exotic, whose mother, I believe, was Japanese. She was slender and dark and gentle, with a long, oval face and beautiful slanting eyes. Her hands were thin and frail, and though she dressed in European clothes, she did not seem to belong to our street at all. I liked them, for even at that early age I was always attracted by oddities and misfits, by people who were in a minority or whom other people looked upon as " foreigners " or " a queer lot." I do not remember the father—perhaps he was a seaman, and away from home a good deal. There was a quietness about the mother and her children which I admired and felt in sympathy with, a good breeding which naturally set them apart from the other people in our street, who may have thought them " stuck-up." There was a certain pride in their reserve, and I think the children were conscious of their difference, but in a philosophic and unassuming way. They were said to be very poor, and to have almost no furniture in their house. No one was ever invited there, and this certainly made them seem even more mysterious. The mother was said to sleep on the floor, on a straw mat. This was looked upon as very peculiar by the housewives of Cockburn Street; I myself thought it rather strange at the time, but my mother and father explained to me that if they were Japanese they would not like to have the same sort of things in their house as we did, and I understood that at once. They liked the mother, and were glad, though I think a trifle anxious, when the children struck up a rather distant friendship with me. I remember being very proud of my strange little friends.

They lived at the very top of the street, at the cemetery end. Their front door was round the corner, in the little back lane, facing the graveyard. There was a rumour that, as they had no beds, the two children were put to sleep in the drawers of a dresser. I thought this was a marvellous idea, and I pleaded hard with my mother to allow me to sleep in a drawer—I could not imagine anything more exciting, more comfortable—but she would never allow it. Nevertheless I often used to pull out a drawer and lie in it fully-clothed for a while, just to prove to myself how sensible it was, and how comfortable, to go to bed in a drawer. My mother didn't like it very much, but I don't think she ever scolded me very severely.

She used to say to me sometimes when a wish of mine had been granted: "Lucky Tully!" And my father would chip in with a gay music-hall song:

Oh, lucky Jim!
How I *envy* him!

Sometimes my mother would say: "You're growing into a spoilt child!" I would have found this very dispiriting if there had not been a mocking inflection in her voice that delighted me, for I knew then that she only half-meant what she was saying, and that though there was perhaps a grain of truth in what she said, my childhood was not altogether irrevocably ruined. I think I got an occasional slap from her, but nothing very serious. Sometimes when I had been naughty she would lift her hand in mock anger, and, looking very fierce, would growl: " I'll bray the living daylights out of ye! " or " You'll get your hammers if you're not careful, me lad! " or " I'll skelp ye, ye little beggor! " I knew that it was all in fun, but I was wise enough to take the hint, too.

My father always said that he would " never lay a hand on me," and he never broke his word. I was grateful to him for that, because I often saw children brutally treated by their parents in our street, and such sights alarmed me more than anything else in those days. My father used to roar with laughter—to the fond exasperation of my mother—whenever she started " playing war " with me. Yet he was properly severe and intolerant in certain matters, and this came from his almost excessive honesty and uprightness. He could be grim, as well as gay, with the grimness of a good man convinced he is in the right. Once he had decided that a thing was in the least bit suspect or shady, nothing would move him to countenance it. He used to impress upon me the need for honesty in my dealings with other people, and for honesty towards myself. More than once he told me the tale of his great-aunt who, if she saw a pin in the street, would not pick it up, because it might not belong to her.

My mother was less inflexible. *She* would certainly have picked up any strange pin she saw lying about and stuck it in her pinafore, saying:

My Father's Side

See a pin and pick it up,
All the day you have good luck!

But though we often felt impatience at what we liked to call " father's stubbornness," we admired and respected him for such undeviating honesty, however eccentric.

My father and mother had a hard life in harsh surroundings, but from early childhood I can remember much laughter and true happiness. They must have taken great pains to conceal from me the financial difficulties they suffered in the 'twenties, a period of distress and misery on Tyneside. Work for joiners in the shipyards and " on the houses " was hard to get. My father was often out of a job, and we lived " on the dole " while he tramped the streets and roads of County Durham with his tool-bag, looking for work. Through constantly carrying his tool-bag from place to place, his right shoulder became permanently lower than the left. He might find employment for a week or two at Consett or Chester-le-Street or Shotley Bridge—how those names haunt me with anxiety still!—and to get there in time he would be up at four or five o'clock in the morning, and would return home, dusty and exhausted, smelling of sawdust and shavings, late in the evening, long after I had gone to bed. Up to the age of five, I was sent to bed every night at six o'clock, though the time was often extended to seven if it was a fine summer evening and if I had " been good." Occasionally when my father came home about eight I would be in bed in the front room but still awake, and he would be able to wish me good night before I went to sleep. How glad I was to see him! Sometimes, to keep her company, my mother would allow me to wait up for him, and however tired he was he would always, after he had washed and

47

eaten, take me on his knee and read to me. Our great dread was to see him come home—if he came home at three o'clock in the afternoon, we knew the worst—his normally fresh-complexioned, healthy face drawn and anxious, with his tool-bag over his shoulder. " Laid off," he would sometimes curtly say. More generally it would be " Paid off."

There was not much pay, either. He had to work hard, and as he was extremely conscientious he probably worked much harder than was necessary. He never earned much more than £3 a week in those days, and it was likely to be much less if frost or bad weather set in and stopped work on the buildings, which he preferred to shipyard work. But he never scamped a job, for he was a good craftsman, and still takes a great pride in his skill.

It was always a struggle to get even the bare necessities of life, and luxuries were " few and far between " as my mother used to say. However hard my parents tried to conceal this struggle from me, I always sensed the strain at the end of the week, when there would be no pennies for the gas, or just enough to buy a two-ounce packet of Brooke Bond's tea at the corner shop. Those were the times when my mother would not answer the Insurance man's knock; we would sit quietly in the kitchen, holding our breath till we heard him go away. This was an exciting game to me, partly because my mother made it so, though it was no joke for her, because she knew there would be double to pay next week.

When I think now of what brave spirit they showed, and of the love and happiness that filled our house in spite of all our difficulties, I feel such gratitude towards my parents, my heart aches with the fullness of my admiration. Such unassuming and devoted courage was not uncommon in the streets of Shields during the " depression." When I think of the long and miserably-paid apprenticeship my father served, and the hardship of his life as a working man, I cannot help feeling resentment at the easier life and higher wages of building workers to-day. I do not begrudge them these better conditions—all men should enjoy freedom and independence and leisure and a worthy, steady wage, and I am proud that my father helped to make such conditions possible. I only regret the bitterness of the struggle, the necessity for so much courage. And I wish he could have enjoyed the fruits of working-class freedom when he was young. The grim days of unemployment on Tyneside in the 'twenties have had mixed results. There is greater health, and, at the moment, greater prosperity among the working classes, and greater leisure, too. But when will they learn to use that leisure fruitfully, creatively? The old pigeon-fanciers and whippet-breeders seem to be a dying race. To-day the working man seems generally lacking in character and initiative, and leads a colourless existence. He is woodenfaced and joyless, his mass-produced life a continual seesaw of hope and disappointment between one week's Pools results and the next. I do not see in his work, either, any of the pride and joy or the sturdy, reliable craftsmanship that my father put into his labour, however poorly paid. The workers, it seems to me, have become the victims of their own revolution.

*   *   **

In the 'twenties many of our neighbours in Cockburn Street were even worse off than we were. A kind of grey despair lay over the town. In our street the men squatted " on their hunkers " outside the front doors or gambled

for " dumpers "—half-smoked Woodbines—in the wash-
ing-hung back lanes. Some of the unemployed gathered
sea-coal on the sands, where it lay in black swathes along
the water's edge after a heavy storm. They would come
home wheeling dripping sacks of it in old perambulators
or slung over the crossbars of broken-down bicycles.
There were long queues at the dreary new " dole office "
in Wawn Street—the very name seemed to make us want
to yawn. Children went barefoot and in rags, begging
for coppers in the streets, while their fathers went on
hunger-marches and their mothers took in washing. I was
lucky: my parents' devotion always provided me with
warm clothes and food, and I never went barefoot, though
they deprived themselves of all kinds of necessities to keep
me well and warm. I believe I was ill only once—with
measles—before I was six.

We made our own amusements then: my mother was
a sweet singer, and sang well songs from *Floridora*, *The
Arcadians* and *The Merry Widow*; and sometimes, to our
great delight, she would entertain us with a few dance
steps—I remember in particular a fascinating can-can
step which she used to perform, a high side-twist to the
leg, like an elevated *rond de jambe*. My father would tell
stories like *Goldilocks and the Three Bears*, and I would
recite all the nursery rhymes I knew or do a dis-
organised little song and dance to the words of lyrics
which I did not understand at all. One went something
like this:

> She's got
> Eyes of blue,
> I never cared for
> Eyes of blue,

My Father's Side

> But *she's* got
> Eyes of blue,
> *That's* my weakness now!

This was followed by " She's got dimpled cheeks," and a whole list of other agreeable attributes with which some fortunate young lady was endowed, and I would sing them all, dancing and jigging away breathlessly all the time. Another, but rather less elegant item in my repertoire was:

> Oh, look at Jimmy,
> Isn't he a seet? (sight)
> With lang, skinny banana legs,
> And umberella feet!

When we were " in funds," there would be occasional visits to " the pictures." We would go to the first house on Saturday, clutching a bag of brazil-nut toffee or chocolate cream whirls, which were my mother's favourite sweet. Sitting on my father's knee in the front row of the Pit at the Queen's, I would chew toffee and gape at the extraordinary " gannins-on " on the screen. I always took the films very seriously—I could never believe that it was " all just a silly story." I can remember only one of the titles of the films I saw before the age of six: it was " Metropolis," and I kept saying the word over and over —I felt it was very grand. Everything that happened on the screen, in that darkened auditorium smelling richly of Jeyes' Fluid, pear-drops, cigarette smoke and orange peel, was a real event to me. The portrayal of wickedness or unhappiness or illness upset me dreadfully, and if the heroine had had a particularly gruelling time in the serial, I would turn to my mother and father for reassurance:

The Only Child

" The lady will be all right now, won't she? " I would ask hopefully, as we walked home up a street whose name appalled me—Mile End Road—because it seemed so desolate, so lacking in comfort, the end of everything.

*   *   *

The river lay just beyond, and could be reached by descending a flight of steep and precarious wooden stairs. But Mile End Road was an " end " in another sense. The railway station was there, as well as the bus and tram terminus.

Sometimes, at week-ends, and particularly on Sunday mornings, my father would take me to see my other grandmother, his mother, and his sister, my Aunt Anna. They lived in a biggish house at Westoe, a rather better-class part of the town, and in order to get there we would board a tram in Mile End Road or Ocean Road and go rattling and shaking up the incline of Fowler Street into the more gradual slope of Westoe Road. The iron tram wheels would be grinding in the tracks, the wooden safety-guards at front and back occasionally clattering on the cobbles as the tram dipped and rolled. There always seemed to be a great number of stops. The cracked bell was always ringing, but sometimes there would be no one waiting at a " request " stop, and we would go surging and swaying on, getting up a fine turn of speed, with the ornamental panels of blue and yellow and ruby glass shivering and chattering and the muffled driver clanking and cranking away in front, his mittened hands on the antiquated controls, his foot pounding the warning bell that was let into the floorboards.

The seats were of hard, ribbed wood or varnished planks with backs that could be swung backwards or

52

forwards according to the direction in which the tram was travelling. Overhead, the trolley would be singing on the electric wire, emitting startlingly vivid blue flashes when its little wheel ran over the joins in the cable. I was fascinated as well as alarmed by these sudden flashes, and often asked for an explanation. " It's the muck " is the only answer I can remember my father giving. We would always ride upstairs, and it was like being on the back of a bird, especially if you sat right up in front, over the driver's head. The trams had open-air platforms upstairs at front and back, and in fine weather the Corporation even brought out vehicles that had no roof at all over the upper part. I shall never forget the fun of riding along in summer sunshine on the packed top deck of a roofless tram, rocking away along Ocean Road, the sea in the distance and the deep blue sky and the humming, lifting and dipping wires sparkling overhead.

But I seem to recall best a journey we made by tram one winter night. We were going to visit my Granny at Westoe, and I was very excited, because an evening excursion was something quite unheard of for me. It had been raining; the gas lamps lit the gleaming pavements and cobbles with a doubled radiance. The shaking tram wires were sending down showers of white raindrops. Everything in the tram seemed fresh and glittering. The breezy windows sparkled with long zig-zags of rain and the passing street lamps gorgeously flared through the panels of blue and yellow and ruby glass. Outside, it was cold and windy, and we could feel the gale buffeting against the side of the tram, making it sway and lurch more than usual, and throwing the passengers against one another. There were bursts of laughter and snatches of song, and the fresh, clean, cold sea-wind was blowing right through the upper deck. Above, a high half-moon seemed to be skidding along on its back through piles of black, white-lined rags. It was a wild night, with a sense of magic in the offing. The people in the tram did not seem like ordinary mortals; a kind of exhilarating gaiety had seïzed them, and it seemed to lighten their bodies and illuminate their faces. At times I was sure we were really flying.

We were sitting, my father and mother and I, in the coveted seat right at the front of the tram, over the driver's head. I was kneeling on the hard, ribbed seat that so satisfyingly corrugated my knees, enjoying the brilliance, the movement, the gaiety, and the glorious feeling of " being up late." We began to grind up the bank, with a sickening, groaning noise that seemed to drag at my bowels, and slowly we rose, past the tree-set hospital, to the Fountain Inn at the top of the hill. This hill is actually a very gentle slope, but to a five-year-old it seemed like a mountain, and the old tram's laboured efforts to get to the top made it appear even steeper than it really was. When we reached the top, the tram had to turn to the right, and this was always a hair-raising manœuvre, for I was sure, every time we turned that corner, that the tram was leaving the rails. What a grinding and griping and jerking there was! I could hardly bear to look at the glimmering rails in front, and yet I *had* to look, in fascinated horror, as the front of the tram seemed to swing right off the track, as if it would never return; but then, slowly, it would nose its way round into the centre of the track again, and I would heave a deep sigh of gratitude for the thrilling moment.

But it was time to get up and make our way down the twisting, slippery metal stairs, clinging to the brass hand-

rail that heaved and shook. Ours was the next stop, at
" The Fountain"—a dismal grey granite horse-trough,
which in those days was the terminus. We clambered
down, and waited to watch the conductor run round the
tram, a hastily-lit fag in his mouth, pulling the chinking
trolley in a wide arc behind him, and setting it, with many
a crackling flash, on the hissing wire, while the driver
drank hot tea from a blue enamel can brought steaming
hot from home by his wife.

Then we went to my Granny Kirkup's house at the top
of Ada Street. It had a small, privet-bordered garden
with ornamental iron railings in front and a squeaky iron
gate. From the outside it looked like a child's drawing
of a house. A big frosted-glass porch stood in the centre,
with a coloured-glass door behind, and on each side of the
porch there was a bay window. On the first floor there
were three windows partnering those below. The walls
were of dingy red brick, the roof was slated, and at
each end of the roof there were chimneys. Near the house,
across a little, narrow cobbled back lane, was a small
police station, which was a great comfort to my nervous
paternal grandmother. The policemen were great friends
of hers, and one of them had given her an old-fashioned,
painted truncheon, which she kept hanging at the foot of
the stairs, in case of burglars.

I can still remember the cold, metal feel of the door
handle as I opened the door of the porch. The outer door
was often swollen by damp, and had to be slammed hard
before it would shut; this caused the whole porch to shake
and rattle like a kaleidoscope. There were several white-
painted shelves inside, on which stood pots of ferns and
mosses and geraniums and other plants. This little con-
servatory was a great delight to me. It smelt always of

autumn and the sea, and on autumn and winter nights it would be full of mist. There was always an odour of damp earth and dead geranium leaves and moist ferns and other growing things. One of the plants was a creeper, which grew from a hanging basket and was called " Wandering Sailor." To me, it was a fine, exotic place, because we had nothing like it at our house. The frosted windows sparkled in the radiance of the red-painted gas-lamp outside the enchanted walls of a snow-palace. Outside, there was a sound of flying slates slicing through the air and crashing on the pavements; but though the strong north-easter made the whole place shiver and leak, it remained inviolable, a draughty haven of glass and greenery, with the comfortable gaslight from the passage glowing through the blue and red panels of the entrance.

Inside, there was a good smell of spicy cooking, jam-making, chinz, minced meat, musty books, coal fires, flowers—generally chrysanthemums—and mint imperials, which my Granny used to suck " for her chest." It was an utterly different smell to the one in our little flat in Cockburn Street, which was a compound of strong tobacco, wood shavings, boiled onions, floor polish and soot. I loved the sweet, old-maid smell of Granny's house, though I always felt that our own was the only right smell for a house to have. I was peculiarly sensitive to the smell of other people's houses. My Granny Johnson's smelt of snuff and shaving soap and boot polish and Woodbines. Mrs. Battey's smelt of washing and hot girdle scones. But most of the houses in our street had the unmistakable, unforgettable smell of poverty—an airless, stuffy, rancid smell, as if the very air, like the tea leaves, had been used over and over again. It was a stale and sour smell of cold, unwashed sheets and bodies, the greasy aroma of pans of vegetable broth, the mustiness of dry crusts, the breath children exhale when they chew dry bread—the very essence of misery.

I sniffed appreciatively at the air in Granny Kirkup's house. She was a genial, plump body with a sweet, rosy, country girl's face. She and her family, the Earls, of Viking stock, had come from Mundesley in Norfolk. My grandfather, her husband, whom I never knew, was of Scots descent, and came from Seaham Harbour. His name was James Falconer Kirkup; he was a captain in the old sailing ships and often made the " China Run " in his tea clipper. Falconer is one of our family names. One of its earlier bearers was the poet William Falconer, a seaman who in 1762 had some literary success with his long poem, in three cantos, called *The Shipwreck*. We are also distantly related to the Barone Seymour Kirkup, friend of Trelawny, Byron, Shelley and Walter Savage Landor. He was a great authority on Dante, and a painter who is best known now for his portrait of Trelawny in fancy dress as Gebir.

My Granny Kirkup was less formidable than my Granny Johnson, though she had the same imperious temper at times. Her large, slightly myopic grey eyes used to twinkle delightfully behind her gold-rimmed glasses, and though she had false teeth, they were so small and white and well made that for many years I did not know they were false. She spoke with a trace of Norfolk accent that I found very agreeable after the broad " Geordie " talk of Cockburn Street. My Granny and my Aunt Anna were strict Methodists, and went regularly to a large, ugly brick chapel called " The Glebe "—a name that I found very perplexing. There was no snuff-taking, gambling or beer-drinking in *this* household, and only weak ginger wine at Christmas and New Year. But there was always a silver threepenny piece hidden in the very slice of cake that my Granny cut for me. " My, my! " she would exclaim. " You'm a lucky crittur! " Now, whenever I read the dialect poems of William Barnes I seem to hear my Granny's rich, country woman's voice. I have never been to Norfolk, but I think there must be similarities between its dialect and that of Dorset, for I clearly remember being astonished and charmed when my Granny said " gurt " for " great " and " wole " for " hole " and " whome " for " home." She also amused me vastly by exclaiming " Lawks! " at the slightest provocation, and using occasional nautical terms borrowed from my grandfather's sailing days. She was terrified of strong winds, which brought back to her bitter memories of storms at sea. The north-east gales seemed to blow very loudly round the house in Ada Street. I used to think of it sometimes as a full-rigged ship labouring in a tempest. This fear and dislike of the wind was transmitted to my father, but not to me.

I have a feeling now that relations between the two " sides " of our family were rather strained; in fact, non-existent. I was only vaguely conscious of this as a child. I remember often longing for the whole family to be together, but they never were. Possibly my mother's family considered my " father's side " to be a pious, stuck-up lot. Pious they were, but never dull; old fashioned, but never bigoted.

I enjoyed my visits to Ada Street; it was like entering a new world. Sometimes on Sunday mornings, when the trams did not start running until lunchtime, my father would take me there in the fat, scarlet " Northern " line buses that ran through Westoe, Harton and Whitburn to Roker and Sunderland. The buses bounced like anything, and their brown leather seats were exhilaratingly springy. But the best thing was the smell of petrol. Petrol fumes were one of my favourite smells, and often if I saw a motor or a van go by the window, I would run out of the house to sniff the rich exhaust aroma before it vanished on the sea-freshened air.

On Sunday mornings at Ada Street I would meet my Granny's lodger, a school teacher at a local girls' school. She was more like a friend of the family than a lodger. She had her own rooms and her own furniture, and she always spoke nicely to me. I was somewhat awed by her, for she " spoke nicely," that is, without any Geordie accent, and she was associated with the dreaded " school " that loomed up ahead of me now that I was nearly five. She had a brightly-painted wooden parrot with a cunningly-weighted tail that swung at the end of her mantelpiece and that I was sometimes allowed to play with. Sometimes her niece from London, a girl rather older than myself, with dark hair cut in a fringe like an " Ovaltine " child, would be staying with her. I was very impressed by the size of the bows she wore in her hair, and by her southern accent. We played together, rather self-consciously, but I remember one hilarious afternoon when we were allowed to slide down the curved lid of Granny's silk-fronted cottage piano. I thought she was very grand, because she was so good at school, and so clever: "brainy" was the word my Granny used. There were lots of books in her aunt's room, and during my schooldays my reluctant respect for books and reading was fostered and developed largely through her keen interest and advice.

The other person I used to meet on Sunday mornings,

after she had come home from " The Glebe," where she sang in the choir, was my Aunt Anna. She was a busy dressmaker and was often out working if we called on a week-day evening. She, too, had short-sighted, large grey eyes, and wore a gold-rimmed pince-nez with a thin gold chain that hooked over one ear. I adored it when she took her spectacles off and wiped them with a neat little folded pocket hanky. Her eyes then appeared even larger, lustrous and vague: they seemed to be looking nowhere in particular, or to be just amiably reposing on dim, far-off things. The strangeness of their expression haunted me, though I also found it rather embarrassing when she removed her glasses: I felt as if I were looking at something I shouldn't see, as if my own sharp eyes were asserting an unfair advantage over her mild, defenceless gaze. Then I would almost tearfully beg her to put her spectacles on again, and until she had finished wiping them I would bury my face in the soft crochet-work of her home-made blouse. Another characteristic that intrigued me was the almost soundless way she blew her nose and sneezed, making no more noise than a little bird. I was so used to my father's impressive trumpetings into his enormous handkerchiefs; I found it very funny when Aunt Anna gave a very lady-like little " cheep " into her tiny, folded hanky, but I believed her when she told me it was not polite to make too much noise when blowing one's nose. My father roared with laughter when I told him that, and said she was quite right, but I noticed that his own sneezes did not become any less earth-shaking.

My Aunt Anna's expression was a little severe, due perhaps to the " Hapsburg " lip which is a prominent feature in all members of the Falconer branch of the family. But she was most wonderfully kind and gentle, and " spoilt " me, and I adored her. We used to go through a ritual on Sunday mornings after she had come back from chapel. She would carry me through the big, Sunday-dinner-smelling kitchen, out into the long, narrow backyard, which I thought was very grand, because they did not have to share it with anyone else. There, with me sitting on her shoulder, we would look up at the telegraph pole that stood in the lane. I would cry " Whee-ee! Whee-ee! Whee-ee! " in imitation of the wind in the wires, and my Aunt Anna, to my intense delight, would cry " Whee-ee! " too. I had never seen anything so tall and impressive as that great giant out in the back lane, covered with struts and little black things like birds. When there were clouds behind it, blowing in from the sea, it would seem to be falling down on us, and we would rush breathlessly back into the house, slamming the door behind us. Then Aunt Anna would let me slide down the curved lid of the silk-pleated piano, and after teaching me some five-finger exercises she would play some of the tunes from " Moody & Sankey's " hymn book. I can still recall the words of one of the hymns:

> Count your blessings, count them one by one,
> And it will *surprise* you what the Lord has done!

Another had a plaintive, and, after the last verse, dramatic refrain: I can't remember the exact words, but it went something like this:

> Passing by! Passing by!
> Jesus of Nazareth *has* passed by!

Another had a good, rollicking tune, and unfortunately the exact words again escape me:

When we meet beyond the morning of that bright and
    happy day,
We shall know each other better, when the mists have
    rolled away!

My irrepressible father used to sing a very sacrilegious
version of this which I found irresistible:

Wash me in the water that you washed your dirty daughter,
And I shall be whiter than the whitewash on the wall!

Then the refrain:

Whi——
ter than the whitewash on the wall,
Whi——
ter than the whitewash on the wall!

Wash me in the water that you washed your dirty daughter,
And *I* shall be whiter than the whitewash on the wall!

  Then we would stand in front of a large dark engraving
of Shakespeare who was depicted sitting meditatively,
dressed in black tights, in a " baronial " chair, with his
creations all around him in a kind of cloudy empyrean,
each wreathed in its appropriate quotation. I believe this
picture was issued by the makers of Pears Soap, which I
did not like because it made my eyes sting, and who
produced a companion picture of a large fat squalling
baby in a tin bath trying to get a tablet of the soap that
lay just beyond his reach: it was entitled " He won't be
happy till he gets it," a saying which was frequently
quoted whenever I wanted something I shouldn't have,
and which became almost a family motto.
  The Shakespeare picture gave me quite a stock of

popular quotations, and often, for the reward of a penny,
I would recite in a whisper of intense loathing:

" Let me not hold my tongue; let me not, Hubert.
   Or Hubert, if you will, cut out my tongue,
   So I may keep mine eyes: O, spare mine eyes! ..."

This picture, the meaningless quotations and the fact
that my own birthday—on 23rd April—fell on the same
day as his, aroused in me at a very early age a keen dislike
of Shakespeare which for a long time I had no desire at
all to overcome.

We would give fresh water to Dick, the canary, whose
cage hung in the bay window of the sitting-room: he
would then take a vigorous bath, chirruping wildly, and
showering us with bird seed and bath-water.

After that, we would look at the needlework picture of
the eighteenth-century boy asleep on a sheep dog; then
she would very conspiratorially open the sideboard drawer
and give me one of Granny's mint imperials while Granny
was out in the kitchen making the dinner. Granny would
pretend not to know what was going on, and when she
came back from the kitchen she would exclaim: " Lawks!
Who's been at my minty sweeties?" I shall not easily
forget the way those mint imperials melted in the mouth
—how the hard, smooth outer casing grew rough and
finally collapsed on one side, releasing the delicious softness of the filling. And I always asked for a glass of cold
water afterwards, because I was a sensationalist, and the
shock of cold water in my peppermint-heated mouth was
one of my first sensuous discoveries.

Then came the best part of the morning, when, among
the smells of roasting meat, cooking vegetables and
stewing apples, my aunt would take me on her knee

and read to me. There was nothing I liked better than being read to. On Saturday afternoons, my father coming home from work would bring in *Bubbles* or *Tiger Tim*, or some other brightly-coloured children's comic, and some chocolate cream whirls. My mother and I would lie down on the sofa after the midday meal, and while my father washed the dishes, we would munch the chocolate cream whirls, and my mother would read the whole of *Bubbles* for me from beginning to end. I would follow her eyes —how blue!—as they moved across the page, and I could always tell when she tried to skip anything. I would stop her then, and insist on hearing every word.

Aunt Anna had a library of " improving " books, some of which I still cherish. There was a copy of the works of Shakespeare in one volume, in tiny, double-columned print on almost brown paper, and old bound volumes of *The Girl's Own Paper*, in which there was a ludicrous *Advice Column for Young Ladies* that was later on to give me much amusement. She had copies of *Chatterbox*, too, full of rather grisly tales: one about *The Woman with Face-ache* gave me some uneasy nights when I was a little older. Another of my favourites was *Little Women*, with its irresistible first line: " Christmas won't be like Christmas without any presents," and its absurd tomboy, Jo March. But the books my Aunt Anna used to read to me on Sundays were tearful, moralising works like *The Lamplighter, The Wide, Wide World, Laddie Tip-Cat, Mrs. Haliburton's Troubles*, and a tiny moral tale by Edna Lyall which I liked best of all, called *Their Happiest Christmas*. This had a label inside saying it was a " prize for attendance " given to my father at Ocean Road Boys' Board School, and signed " P. Murray, Head Teacher." At the top of the label was the South

My Father's Side

Shields coat-of-arms—a lifeboat surmounted by an anchor, with the words " Always Ready." The tale was a " lesson in unselfishness," and I still seem to hear my aunt's rather throaty, squeaky voice as she read the opening lines:

" I hate you, Joan! You're the spitefullest, crossest sister in the world! "

" And so are you the crossest brother! "

So began the story of Jack and Joan Radcliffe and of how they were taken by burly, bearded Cousin Paul, a nice big-brother type, to a children's hospital on Christmas Day, and gave presents to all the little patients. I never tired of this delightful tale, and asked for it over and over again, at least until I was about seven, when I began to distrust " preachy " stories.

When the reading was finished, it would be time for my father and me to leave and go back to Cockburn Street, where my mother was " on with the dinner." And off I would go to the tram stop, with another mint imperial in my mouth, after kissing Granny and Aunt Anna— something I never liked doing, for I only liked kissing my mother and father. It was horrible to have to kiss other people. I don't think I ever stayed to dinner at Ada Street on Sundays, possibly because I always used to refuse to eat anything that had not been cooked by my mother. Other people's food used to make me sick. I always dreaded being taken out to tea or dinner, and having to eat other people's messes. We had a good, plain diet at home: mostly roast beef, Yorkshire pudding and vegetables, generally followed by rice pudding or tinned fruit. I never found it monotonous. Sometimes, as a great treat, we had tinned salmon. I am always surprised when I read about the loathing that most children seem to feel for rice pudding.

The Only Child

Any departure from this very narrow bill-of-fare upset and I think rather frightened me. I remember being very distressed when my mother, hoping to make it more nourishing, one day put an egg in the rice pudding. The sort of meals other people made always seemed to me thoroughly strange and nasty, and perhaps my lack of interest in food dates from those early experiences at outlandish tables.

4. *The Back Yard*

THE PORTRAIT of our house in Cockburn Street would not be complete if I did not say something about the backyard, and the back lane outside it. Even in those days, when house and street and door and window seemed to me enormous, I felt the backyard was a poky place, so I suppose it must have been very small. It was overshadowed by our one-storied house with its steep slate roof and ugly chimneys, and by the cat-stalked dividing walls and outhouses. It was dark, and cold, for the back of our house faced north-east, and got no sun; when it was fine weather, the front got the sun all day long, and sometimes we had to pull down the yellow paper blind over the " room " window or else the little front parlour became unbearably hot and stuffy. But it was always cool, and dim, in the back room and the scullery; often, in winter, we had to have the gas burning all day long.

Two rain-water barrels stood in our backyard—one was ours, one was Mrs. Battey's—and these collected the sooty rain water that flowed from the roof. The sides were tarred, and covered with huge blisters. I soon discovered the pleasures of blister-bursting: I would press a finger-nail on a good, fat blister until the skin of paint burst, and a trickle of faintly oily liquid spurted out. " The tubs," as they were called, had wooden covers to prevent soot and dirt falling into the water. Occasionally, when my mother or father was drawing a dishful of rain water, I would be lifted up to look over the edge of the tub. How black the water looked, how deep, still, and cold! How my voice boomed when I spoke with my head hanging over that black well, and how dark my pale face looked down there, swimming in a white-reflected sky, ash-blond curls blown dark as the grey clouds! It was an awe-inspiring sight, one that I half-dreaded, half-desired to look upon. It made me think of drowning, of my father's tales about the sea, of those great-grandfathers and great-uncles who had been lost at sea. I dreaded the sight of the black water in those tubs far more than the sea. I did not take much notice of the sea until I was about six. I took it for granted, like a grown-up whom one has always known.

The blackness of those tubs seemed even blacker than the blackness of the coal-house, their coldness colder than the green-distempered chill of the " closet " that was emptied once a week, at dead of night, by the scavengers with a horse and cart. I recall waking up at night and hearing the sound of the scavenger's cart rumbling slowly over the cobbles of the back lane; I could hear, as in a disordered dream, the snortings and stampings of the impatient horse, and the lowered voices of the men as they shovelled the night soil out of the middens, whose small iron doors, that gave on to the back lane, they slammed with muffled oaths. . . . They were strange beings, those unknown men toiling at their lowly task. No one ever knew who they were: they preferred to work at dead of night so that their identities would not be discovered. Some said they were convicts, and some children I knew said they came up out of the sea, or out of the harbour round the Black Rocks each night to do their dirty work. I thought of them, not as ordinary men, but as " bogles " or bogey-men; they were black giants, but I was sure they would be kind to me if I met them in a dark lane, at dead of night. Some children with foolish parents were told that if they were naughty the scavengers would come and take them away at night in their stinking cart. It was surely very cruel, I felt, to say such things to one's own little boy and girl.

A few years later, I was to learn this quaint little rhyme about the scavengers from one of my school-fellows:

> My father's a midnight mechanic,
> He works in the middens by night,
> And when he comes home in the morning,
> He's covered with Turkish Delight.

Sung to a simple little tune, this song so obsessed me that I sang it to myself for days and days; it just stuck in my mind and nothing would get it out, and in the end the words became quite meaningless: only the charm of the melody remained. But one Sunday at lunchtime I suddenly found myself singing the words at table as my mother was serving the vegetables. After a moment of shocked horror as the full realisation of what the song meant and of the enormity of my unthinking action dawned upon me, my mother and father, to my relief, were overcome by paroxysms of mirth, in which I eventually joined, though I still felt very shame-faced. But I had finally got the awful song out of my system and was able to enjoy my dinner that day.

But that was four or five years later, when I had begun to lose some of my almost pathological innocence—about the time when, to my infinite regret, I had to stop believing in Father Christmas. I must get back to our backyard as it appeared to me between the ages of two and three, when I really began to " sit up and take notice " of what was going on around me.

The ground out in the backyard was made of a kind of coarse concrete, full of tiny shells and pebbles—shingle from our sands. The little stones, worn smooth by the pounding of the North Sea breakers, had been made even smoother by the passage of countless colliers' boots and housewives' shoes. The stones were mostly brown in colour, but there were also yellow and black and white and striped ones, and others that were the brown-blue shade of a ripe black eye; there were also well-rubbed fragments of old brick, and bits of green, dull bottle-glass, both pale and dark. These, with jagged portions of broken shells, were all conglomerated in a hard, smooth, cement-roughened mass that looked dull when dry but shone and sparkled when it rained or when my father or Mr. Battey " scrubbed the yard "—a weekly ritual— with great pailfuls of tap-water and a stiff-bristled yard broom. I had soon noticed, on the beach, how stones and shells and seaweed shone when they were wet, and how disappointingly dull they were when dry. Our backyard was like having a section of the beach on our own scullery doorstep—but fixed, and hard, and immovable, despite the great tides of tap-water my father regularly sluiced over it.

Among all these variegated pebbles there was one that stood out. It was in a dark corner of the yard, near Mrs. Battey's green-painted coal-house door. This pebble was

The Back Yard

slightly smaller than the rest, but it was bright scarlet. It was the only one of its kind, and its brilliant red had earned it the name of " The Bloodstone." It certainly was not a real bloodstone, which is dark green, flecked with red. Nor could it possibly have been a ruby, or a cat's eye, as some asserted, for it was opaque. It was most mysterious. Children used to come from near and far, lifting the " sneck " of our back door, and shouting: " Mrs. Battey! Mrs. Kirpick! " (they could never get our name right); " can we come in and see the Bloodstone? " They would come in and stand or crouch in a silent, awestruck ring round the little crimson stone. Some adventurous soul might try to dig it out with a pen nib or a penknife, and my heart, as I stood watching them from the kitchen window, would contract with anxiety; but nothing would shift it; the children would stare at it and discuss it in hushed whispers, nodding their heads with " old-fashioned " seriousness. It gave great renown and distinction to our backyard, and though I went very much in awe of the Bloodstone, I was very proud of it. I always treated it with great respect—I would never have dreamed of *walking* on it, for example—and I fully believed it had magic properties, though I never wished to test them, for I was sure that any sort of magic would be unpleasant and alarming.

Many were the tales and prohibitions it inspired. Some said it was the tooth out of a Chinese donkeyman's head, and others that a coalman had spat it out, red-hot. Some said it was a " bogle." Now on Tyneside a " bogle " was something one picked out of one's nose, but it could also be something spooky. Romantic-minded little girls said it was a queen's finger-nail, and indeed it had the shape and size of a delicate little finger-nail. But the boys of

71

course scoffed at this idea. Some said it was a scarlet
bean, that sprouted diamonds once every hundred
years. Some swore it was giant's blood. But all were
agreed that it was fatal to stand on it, or to touch it, unless
you had spat on it first. If you were to touch it without
spitting on it, you would drop down dead, or your finger
would fall off. I can still see a little circle of crouching
backsides—tightly-stretched little breeches and knickers
—sometimes no knickers at all—and potato-holed stockings gathered round the Bloodstone, and can hear that
chorus of infant spitting as they made the stone safe to
touch.

One day, playing on my own in the backyard, in the
chill shadow of the coalhouses and the rain-water tubs,
I suddenly realised, as I crawled over the palm-denting
ground, that I had inadvertently put my hand on—the
Bloodstone! A shudder of fright went through me as I
slowly lifted my hand and revealed the terrible stone—
smooth, sinister, brilliant, like an open wound that can
never be healed. It was a feeling much worse than when
you put your hand in " mess " or in a dog's " business "
or on one of the great, shining half-crowns of spit that
illuminated, with a grisly radiance, the dark kerbs of the
front street. I went cold, and my hand seemed to burn
where the stone had touched it. I sat there, unable to
warn my mother, who was singing happily as she worked
in the scullery; I couldn't make a sound: I just couldn't
bring myself to tell her that I was about to drop dead.

I saw the whole yard very clearly—the tall brick walls
that led up dizzily to the dark-blue sky, the broken clouds,
the smoke from the river drifting faster than the moving
clouds, the seagulls smoothly rocking in the wind from
the sea. I saw the swollen blisters—there were several

new ones—on the sides of the rain-water barrels, and longed to burst some of them. I reached out and burst a big, juicy one, then another, and another and another. The familiar oily, tarry smell came from them. By the time I had burst half a dozen I began to admit to myself that though I had touched the Bloodstone without spitting on it first, I had not dropped down dead. Cautiously, I spat on the Bloodstone, just for luck . . . better late than never. Then I got up and ran to my mother and flung myself into her arms. Even she, who was used to my successive attacks of paralysed shyness and wild demonstrativeness, was puzzled by my outburst of tears and laughter. I couldn't tell her what had happened. But just as I had known at once what ghosts were, so at that moment in the backyard I knew what death would be like—an unspeakable moment of realisation which we can share with no one, for the shock of knowledge takes us out of ourselves, and puts us far away, on our own, lonelier than ever, and far beyond the reach even of those we know and love best.

5. The Back Lane

EACH DAY of the week had its own activity, its own special atmosphere, as distinct and unalterable as Sunday. Nowadays housewives no longer have such a rigidly-planned week, perhaps rightly so; but I am always uneasy when I see washing being hung out on a Wednesday or baking being done on a Saturday. It seems all wrong; it's as if the stars had changed their courses.

Sunday was the day of rest, though only of comparative rest for my mother, who had all the cooking to do. But there was an atmosphere of quiet contentment on Sunday after tea, broken only by the fall of red-hot ashes into the grate and the gentle rustling of tired Sunday papers.

Tuesday was ironing day, with sheets and lace window curtains and shirts and underclothes airing on the clothes-horse in front of the fire or hanging from clothes-lines stretched across the kitchen ceiling. This gave a rather oppressive feeling. But there were wonderful moments when my mother and I folded sheets and tablecloths and blankets—performing a sort of ritual ballet of opening and closing arms, of advancing and retreating steps. Another amusing activity was the " stretching " of the lace window curtains; these long, white draperies were stiff and rough before we set to work on them. My mother would take hold of one end, and I would grasp the other as tightly as I could, and then, standing on opposite sides of the kitchen, we would pull and tug—sometimes my mother pulled so hard that I was tugged off my balance—until the rough lace had become well stretched, soft and limp. It did not " drape " well if we did not " tussle " it.

Wednesday was baking day. My mother made a big batch of loaves, " oven-bottom " cakes, currant scones, shortbread and rice cakes. I would be allowed to make a " dough-man," with currant buttons and eyes and nose and mouth; he was always very grubby by the time I had finished making him, but the little grey doll would be popped into the oven with the scones. He was eaten hot, and although I was proud of my baking, I never really thought he tasted nice. I would watch my mother mixing the flour for the bread, and kneading it in a big bowl into dough which was set in front of the fire to " rise." When it had risen, it was divided up into four parts and put into bread tins; my mother " progged " the top of the loaves in an interesting pattern with a kitchen fork, and then left them in front of the fire a little longer before putting them into the oven. What happy, rich-smelling days those baking days were!

Thursday was mending day, when my mother darned socks and patched shirts and trousers and dungarees. I used to try my hand at darning, but I was never very successful at it; nor did I fare any better at knitting, though I made painful efforts to get it right. I can see myself now, poring over a few rows of rough, lumpy plain and purl, chanting absorbedly to myself the slow litany of instructions: " In, over, through, *off*, in, over, through, *off*." We also used to make " clippy " mats with rag

clippings. Sacking—" harn," we called it—was stretched
on a set of mat frames; a hole was made in the harn with
a wooden " progger," and a clipping was pushed through
and brought up through another hole at the side of the
first. I remember vividly the smell of the fresh harn, that
used to make me sneeze, and the lovely softness of a
newly-finished rug. It was a laborious process, but everyone, including friends, neighbours and relations, lent a
hand, and I enjoyed mat-making because it was a real
social event.

Friday I disliked, because it was cleaning day. Everything was dusted and polished, and the floors were
scrubbed. The mats were taken up at night, and beaten
in the back lane, because it was illegal to beat them during
the day. The hearth was freshly whitewashed and black-
leaded, and the brass fire-irons and the fender were
polished with " Meppo " or " Zebra " metal polish. Our
old brass candlesticks would be taken down from the high
mantelpiece and polished too. I thought it was like magic,
the way the tarnished brass, coated with grey liquid,
turned a new, brilliant gold. We would polish the cutlery,
too, with pink powder, and among the cutlery were my
own two personal pieces—a spoon and a " pusher "; the
latter was an inelegant little implement which I used
to push food on to my spoon. I would much rather have
had a proper knife and fork, but I was not allowed to use
these until I was five.

Saturday was shopping day, because it was the day
Father brought his pay packet home, when he was
working. I loved delving into my mother's shopping-bag
when she came back from the shops, looking among such
dull things as salt and flour and " Robin " starch and
soda and " Jolly-washer " soap and matches and " blue "

bags for the little twist of boiled sweets—generally orange drops—which the grocer used to slip in free with every weekly order.

Monday, of course, was washing day. It started early, often before daybreak, with my mother filling the " copper " in the washhouse and lighting the fire beneath it. When I got up for my breakfast, I would be depressed by the piles of dirty linen which she had already sorted out on the kitchen floor. She would be in her oldest clothes, wearing a pair of old shoes and no stockings, and with a scarf tied round her head; as on baking days, her sleeves would be rolled up well above the elbows, showing her firm, strong arms that would soon be gloved with suds. In the washhouse we had a huge, antiquated mangle which I tried to help her to turn. Washing-lines would be wiped and hung across the back lane while the dirty clothes were boiling in the copper. Sheets and blankets and tablecloths would be " possed " in a " poss-tub " or " posser " with a heavy wooden " poss-stick." I liked the hollow, rhythmical, drumming noise my mother made with the poss-stick on the bottom of the poss-tub. She sang cheerfully and made the suds fly gaily over the edge of the poss-tub. The steam would rise in great clouds, smelling of soda and blue-mottled soap, round her pink face and damp fair hair. It was hard work, but she set about it with a gay, dashing energy, hauling heavy, soaking-wet blankets out of the tub and wringing them easily with her strong, capable hands. By dinner-time, the heaviest part of the job was over, and we would sit down to a lunch of cold meat and bread and butter and tea, with the washing all pegged out, waving and drying in the back lane. It was a satisfying moment.

Though we washed only on Mondays, there always

seemed to be washing hanging outside the neighbours' back doors in our little back lane. It would be pegged out with smooth, worn pegs bought from an old gipsy woman who wandered the back lanes of Tyneside and who was known as the " prop-wife," because in addition to carrying over one arm a great wicker basket full of pegs she would have over her shoulder half a dozen eight-foot clothes-props, rough lengths of timber, notched at one end, which were used to hoist the clothes-lines into the air when the wet washing had been pegged out on them. The prop-wife used to go through the lanes calling:

" Props! Any props! Props! Any pegs, hinney? Pegs a penny a pair! "

At the sound of her voice, children would run out of the houses and the backyards and follow after her, shouting " Props! Props! " and pulling at her black wool-lace shawl and her long, trailing black skirts. We were half-frightened of her, for her face was tanned and weather-beaten like a witch's, her smooth, coiled black hair had never known a hat, and she had an extensive vocabulary of swear-words. When the " kids " became too daring, she would round on them, and they would listen with shocked delight to the stream of filth and abuse that poured from her toothless mouth. Or if she were in a less cantankerous mood she would lock two pegs together, hold them as if they were a pistol, and pretend to shoot us all, spitting out chewed tobacco, working her thick black eyebrows with terrifying effect, and shouting:

" Bang-bang! Bang-bang! Ye're deed, the f—— lot o' ye's."

She was sometimes accompanied by an immensely tall, thin, fierce-looking man—some said he was her father, some her husband—who would come carrying a dozen props over each shoulder, and shout:

"Aa'm back! Aa'm back in canny ould Shields! Props, hinney? Tanner a piece, hinney, Aa'm on the beor."

When "us kids" got too cheeky, the prop-wife in exasperation would strike out at our legs with a prop, over which we would jump as if over a skipping-rope. But when *he* was with her we never dared to tease the prop-wife. My mother never allowed me to run after the prop-wife and call her names as the other children did; in fact, I don't think I would ever have wanted to, for we looked upon her as a poor, pathetic, half-crazed creature. But the old girl was a part of every wash-day.

I shall never forget the feeling of misery a wash-day brought. It always upset me to see things topsy-turvy in our little house; for wash-day the clippy mats were rolled up, the kitchen table stripped and a big black metal pan of rain-water put to boil on the fire—what a sooty smell the steam from it had when it was taken off! Of course, things were a lot worse when it was bad weather and our kitchen was clammy with damp washing hanging from the ceiling and from the clothes-horse in front of the fire. But when it was sunny or breezy—a good drying day— everything would be hung out in the back lane, where it was at the mercy of "soot flights" and "kiddars" with dirty fingers and—the coalman with his cart.

There was an enchantment in all the sopping sheets and clothes and blankets stretched across the back lane in the wind and sun. What a scamper there was to bring them inside if it started to rain! In spite of their being hoisted up by the props, the heavy clothes would hang almost to the cobbles, and I would wander, as if in a magical labyrinth, among the tall, wet, swaying walls of wool and cotton with their dank and soapy smell of sunny steam. Sometimes I would almost get lost in those great blank, narrow alleys of clammy whiteness, and then it was always a relief to see my mother's comfortable shadow on a sunlit sheet, her arms raised to the line, her head lifted and her mouth full of pegs. On really sunny days, the sheets made a brilliant maze that it was fun to hide in. I can still feel, like a soft, ghostly hand, the faintly-chill touch of a damp and breeze-blown blanket on my cheek and brow.

The cry of the coalman would be heard at the end of the back lane:

" Co-al! Beany Co-al! Co-al, tanner a bucket! Beany co-al! "

At this hoarse cry, all the housewives in the street would rush out of their back doors to hold back their sheets like theatre curtains or to " furl their sails "—that is, to peg their washing high up on the lines so that the coalman and his horse and cart could pass underneath without smutching it. It was always a small tip-up cart with a load of small coal, and the coalman and his horse would duck their coal-dusted heads under the furled sheets and shirts. There was great consternation when the coalman tipped his cartload outside somebody's coalhouse hatch, for this sent up clouds of coal dust. There was a lot of good-humoured banter from the women as the coalman slowly moved from back door to back door.

" Howway, hinney! " he would shout. " Let we get by —Aa hevvn't aal day te stand taakin."

" Howway then ye dorty ould beggor," the housewife would shout, " divven't mucky me claes, or Aa'll gi' ye watt foor."

The Back Lane

" Aal reet, hinney, dain't fash yerself, Aa'm gannin," the coalman would reply.

" Aa dain't knaa watt ye want to cum roond of a Monda'—ivvery week the syem, ye ould beggor ye! "

" Wey if ye dain't want ony beany coal missus Aa'll haddaway."

" Aye, haddaway afore Aa croon ye one."

However angry they sounded, they were always good humoured; somewhere in the lane, in spite of his un-welcome appearance, the coalman would be given a cup of tea, and his horse a carrot or a sugar-lump, for Tyneside people are well known to be the most friendly, good-natured and hospitable people in the world. And the coalman would move away grinning, and saying:

" Wey, aye, hinney, thes na place like canny ould Shiels." And the coal cart, its scales swinging from the back-board, would slowly rattle away over the soap-sudded cobbles and disappear behind the row-on-row of prop-peaked washing lines, and we would hear more sounds of argument and laughter mingling with the clatter of zinc buckets and iron shovels and the roar of tipping coals coming from the other end of our lane, but growing fainter and fainter as he progressed from one cup of tea to the next, till they were muffled and lost behind the heaving wilderness of other folks' blankets and sheets and combinations and Union shirts and knickers and nappies and towels and nightdresses and tablecloths and curtains and dungarees—a strangely-populated country of billowing, disembodied vests and pants.

There were other passers-by in our back lane, of course, but they took care not to come on washing day; only the popular and indispensable coalman could get away with that.

The fishwife, wearing a man's cap with a hatpin in it, and a pad on top, on which she balanced her fish basket, and with a scaly blue apron or a sack tied over an old trench-coat, would come striding down the lane on Fridays shouting:

" Fi-ish! Ony fi-ish? Mackerel! Fine finney haddey! Fr-resh fish! Ony crabs? Fine kippered herring! Fi-ish! Ony fi-ish? " And the housewives would run out with a plate and a teacloth. How red-raw the fishwife's hands looked, as she chopped a slice of cod, or gutted a red herring with her sharp, worn knife that glittered in the sun! She was a mysterious, silent woman who rarely accepted a cup of tea. All that could be got out of her was the price of fish, so it seemed very strange when, after serving us without a word, she suddenly burst out with her raucous hawker's cries. Apart from her alpaca shirt, she seemed to wear only men's clothes, including big sea-boots.

Another back-lane figure was the rag-and-bone man, with his jam jars and bundles of old clothes, his rusty tin baths and old brass bedsteads. He wore a battered top hat, and would occasionally oblige with a step dance and a completely unintelligible song. He was said to be very wealthy.

A less picturesque character was the fruit man. I do not remember much about him except his almost meaning-less cry:

" Apples a pound pears! "

But who could forget the colourful splendour of his cart piled with all kinds of fruit? There were pyramids of rosy apples and oranges; bananas, tomatoes, pome-granates, grapes, as well as potatoes, carrots, cauliflower, cabbage and—rhubarb, which I hated, but which I was made to eat because it was supposed to " cool the blood." I didn't want my blood cooled—there was a gruesome sound about it. He also sold bunches of old-fashioned flowers from the miners' allotments—Sweet William, Marguerites, Wallflowers, Pansies, "Chrysanths," Golden Rod, Asters, Dahlias, Lupins, Dusty Millers, Michaelmas Daisies and Southron Wood. I think it was from him, too, that we bought " liquorice sticks "—rough, woody, insipid roots that tasted vaguely of liquorice and went all stringy when they were chewed. His nuts were lovely, particularly those very small, sweet, wrinkled ones we called " Tiger Nuts." Some children bought from him ha'porths of a nasty-looking brown stuff called, if I remember rightly, " Locusts." I don't know what it was, nor why it was given that name. But it looked to me like " caca," and I would never eat it.

There was the knife-grinder with a strange contraption, all wheels and belts and whirling grindstones. It was worked by a foot-pedal. He would lay a carving-knife or a pair of scissors most sensitively, as if he were an artist, across his whirring grindstone, and the sparks would fly from under his hands. Then, the job finished, he would pick up the contraption by two handles and wheel it away like a perambulator. Very occasionally, an old chair-mender would come round with him, but I don't think he could have found much work in our neighbourhood.

There was a sharp distinction between the people who used the back lane and those who used the front street to sell their wares. The milkman, for example, was a " cut above " the fruit man, and never sold his milk in the back lane. He would ride down the street with his great brass-labelled churn swinging between the sparkling, prettily-painted wheels of the milk float; he would ring a hand-

bell, shouting " Mi-ilk! Milko! " and I would go out
with a flowered jug and wait, holding it out carefully,
while he plunged his half-pint measure into the churn and
brought it up dripping and foaming, and frothed it into
the jug. He was a devil-may-care young fellow, with a
straw boater always on the back of his brilliantined head
and a village rose in his horse's headband. He would give
a flick of his long whip, leap whistling on to the back step
of the float, and off he would clatter down the cobbled
street—his rosy cheeks a memory of seaside fields and
farms on the edges of cliffs.

Then there was the tea man—Lipton's Tea. I remember his smartly-painted, black and green, high, elegant
horse-drawn vehicle that looked almost like a gipsy's
caravan. When he opened the big doors at the back,
there were piles of plump, different-coloured packets of
tea inside—pink, blue, white, yellow and green packets,
all at different prices.

I'm not sure, but I believe I remember an old muffin-
man calling his wares in the twilight of a winter evening
in the foggy front street. Certainly there was a lamplighter, with his tiny flame flickering at the end of a long
pole, who went from lamp to lamp lighting the gas. I
often used to watch him thrust his pole through the
aperture in the bottom of the gas lamp and pull down a
lever; then the gas mantle lit with a subdued *plop*. He
was a romantic, harassed figure. I always felt worried
about him, for he was always in such a hurry, and I
thought he had to light all the hundreds of street lamps
in South Shields—I felt that he should be wearing a
nightgown, like Wee Willie Winkie, as he ran through
the town.

There were many newspaper sellers, many of them

The Back Lane

small children, who ran through the streets crying
" *Sporting Ma-an!* " or " *Shields Gazette! Gazette!* " I
longed to sell newspapers, but was not allowed to. I wasn't
even allowed to have a delivery round, to my bitter regret.
But all that came years later, when I was at the " Big
Boys' School."

Some of the street calls were almost like songs, and the
pattern of the words never varied. They were a part of
daily life. I can still sing the ragman's " Ony rags,
bottles or bones? Ony jam jars? " and the fishwife's
" Kippered Herring," and the fruit man's " Buy rhubarb,
buy rhubarb! Buy rhubarb, buy rhubarb! "

6. Songs and Singers

STREET SINGERS were real entertainers in those days, when wireless was rare and " the pictures " could be afforded only once a week at the most.

There were three classes of street entertainers. First came the instrumentalists: they were " top of the bill " in any street. There was the old white-haired, respectable gentleman in a wide-brimmed black hat—looking, I now realise, exactly like the destitute violinist in the Musicians' Benevolent Fund advertisements—who used to stand outside the larger stores and scrape tunelessly away, interrupting the " melody " from time to time to accept a coin and a word of sympathy with a courtly bow. There were also young cornet players—unemployed miners, ex-Army or ex-Boys' Brigade—who used to " render " sentimental songs like *I'm Forever Blowing Bubbles* and *Golden Dreamboat* with excruciating slowness as they wandered slowly down the middle of the front street, turning pleadingly from side to side as they played, hoping to hear the chink of paper-wrapped coppers thrown on the pavements, and with a wary weather eye open for the copper or the " slop."

Mouth-organ players were very common, and so were

concertina and melodion virtuosi. They would generally station themselves at the doors of pubs and break into a wheezy *Alexander's Ragtime Band* or *Felix Kept on Walking* or *Lily of Laguna* while the pianist inside was knocking back his pint of black-and-tan. In this class, too, was the tittupping, hiccuping barrel organ that seemed to spray the air with sudden sprinkling rushes of notes, and paused in the middle of a bar while the organ grinder picked a copper out of the gutter. Then it would carry on, very fast, in a strange *tempo rubato*, as if making up for lost time, with *If You were the Only Girl in the World*. The little girls used to dance round it, lifting up their pinnies and their frocks, just like a Phil May drawing.

Next there came the singers. There was a striking, tall, middle-aged woman, accompanied by a little girl to pick up the pennies, who used to sing, in a piercingly accurate soprano, *Jerusalem*, or *I Dreamt that I Dwelt in Marble Halls*. The women in our street used to shake their shawled heads over her, with sympathetic envy, it seems to me now. They all said she was a " lady " who, through no fault of her own, but because of the drunken habits of a rich and dissolute husband, had fallen on hard times. They said she could make a fortune " on the Empire," and I often used to wonder why she didn't if she was so poor. I was once sent out with a penny to give to her little girl, in the middle of an ear-splitting rendition of *The Old Folks at Home*. I felt very small and embarrassed, with the eyes of the whole street upon me. The woman's presence made itself powerfully felt—a shiver went over me as I approached her. There was something extraordinarily moving about her—her great height, her sad and noble face, her dark, lustrous eyes, the man's coat and cap she wore and the passion she put into her singing filled me with awe. Just as I was giving the penny to the thin, dark-eyed girl with her long, straight black hair, the woman stopped, on a particularly piercing note, bowed her head to me—it was the very slightest of acknowledgements, but even so it seemed too much—and said, in a ripe Geordie accent: " Bless ye, me canny lad! " She immediately went on singing, scooping up to the high note where she had left off, and gazing soulfully up at the windows. A distinct smell of spirits hung around her, and at such close quarters I could see she was dirty and black-toothed; the little girl smelt funny, too. Infant though I was, I realised she was not everything she appeared to be from the neighbours' romantic accounts. I ran back, hot with shame, to our house, where my mother and my Granny Johnson were watching me from behind the front-room lace curtains, and said breathlessly:

" She's *not* a lady, Mam, she smells like Granny! " This caused great merriment, in which I joined, though I didn't know why. " Wise bairn! " said my Granny, wiping her eyes.

The other street singers I remember were all men— some of them young, workless and hungry, who sang in high, light tenor voices *The Minstrel Boy* or *Charmaine* or *When the Red, Red Robin Comes Bob-Bob-Bobbin' Along*. They were pathetic, and were given cups of tea as well as pennies, and old shoes and jackets. One of them had a fine Irish brogue, and my mother and I would listen to his "blather" with the greatest delight. There were also the middle-aged and old men who sang: sad relics of a former respectability—an overcoat with a velvet collar that had seen better days, a well-waxed moustache, or even, in one case, a monocle and greasy suède shoes— told us that they, too, had " come down in the world."

Songs and Singers

They would sing gallant soldier ditties like *Tipperary*, *There's a Long, Long Trail A-Winding*, or sad modern songs like *Stormy Weather* and *Show Me the Way to Go Home*. If they were very old, they would give us *Two Little Girls in Blue*, *Grandfather's Clock*, and, seedily-debonair, *The Man Who Broke the Bank at Monte Carlo* or *A Batchelor Gay am I*, the last being often accompanied by a rather breathy, yodelling step dance, in which there was always a lot of " business " with an umbrella and old top-hat. The housewives standing on their front-door steps with folded arms would all agree that they were " a proper scream," but that it was " a shame."

Lastly, there were the drunks, who always sang, and who always used the back lane. They were not real entertainers; they were looked down upon by the " regulars " or " legitimates " and they got very little sympathy from their unwilling listeners. They would raise their voices in the afternoon, after closing time, and we would be treated to the most awful caterwauling versions of *Nellie Dean*, *The Old Rustic Bridge by the Mill*, and *Just a Song at Twilight*. I was never allowed to go out and give them pennies, though I often wanted to, when they seemed to be in a particularly bad way. Their whooping, sluggish, disembodied voices, floating with painful clarity over our backyard wall, used to move me to tears. But my sensible mother would have none of it. " Divven't be se daft," she would tell me, using a broad Geordie accent to make me laugh, and with the usual hint of gentle mockery in her voice. " They're mebbe a lot better off than we are," she would add. But she would make me tea and toast, to console me, and we would sit by the fire to have it, with our feet up on the warm metal fender, while I pondered over the harshness of the world and wondered if I should ever have to sing for pennies in the back streets. Then I would climb happily on her lap, and fall asleep while she whispered softly, her cheek next to my own tear-stained one:

> Be-ba, bunting,
> Daddy's gone a-hunting,
> Gone to get a rabbit-skin
> To wrap wee Baby Bunting in.

7. *Rhymes and Fancies*

I ALWAYS took great delight in the songs, catches and rhymes I learned from my mother and father, and " the kids round the doors." One of my very first memories is connected with a dancing rhyme which the little girls in our street used to sing. I must have heard it sung from my tenderest years, but I never bothered about the meaning of its incomprehensible jingle; I was content to sit in my pram and listen to the words. I remember sitting on our front doorstep—I must have been no more than two years old at the time—and watching a crowd of girls dancing in a ring round the lamp-post near our door, singing the rhyme at the tops of their voices. I was a little uneasy about the whole display—something rather wild about the words and the abandon of the dancing faintly shocked my infant primness; and on the final word, the girls all lifted up their frocks at the back and shoved their bottoms out in a way which I found very distressing. The words went something like this:

> Halligal, eagle, eagle,
> Halligal, eagle, ee!
> Halligal, eagle, eagle,

The Only Child

Upon a Sarrada' neet
Whee!

But even the harmless *Ring-a-ring-a-roses* seemed improper to me in those days, because of the sneezes and all the falling down: I was always upset by things falling down—it distressed me if a glove fell on the floor or a chair was knocked over. And whenever I joined in with other children playing *Ring-a-ring-a-roses*—that rarely happened—I always refused to fall down at the end. I felt obscurely that it was " not right."

The rhymes and songs I enjoyed in the safety of our house with my mother and father for playmates were very much more to my taste, though I couldn't help thinking that some of them were extremely odd. Dancing me up and down on her knees, with my hands safely clasped in hers, my mother would chant:

> Diddle diddle dumpling,
> My son John
> Went to bed with his trousers on.
> One shoe off
> And one shoe on,
> Diddle diddle dumpling,
> My son John.

I used to take this rhyme very seriously. Whenever I heard it, I felt sure that my mother had another son hidden away somewhere who was called John. Though he was obviously podgy, I longed to see this brother, and ask him why he did such odd things. I couldn't imagine anything odder than going to bed with one's trousers on, but if brother John could do it, I reasoned, with the down-to-earth logic of a child, why couldn't I? But my mother would never let me go to bed with my trousers on. As for John's having one shoe off and one shoe on, I felt that there must be something seriously wrong somewhere: my mother was not taking proper care of him, I thought, though I did not tell her so. The rhyme said he did these silly things, so it must be true. I tried walking with one shoe off and one shoe on, and found it very disagreeable. What a strange, interesting brother this dumpling John must be! I longed to meet him and to ask him to explain himself. But whenever I asked to see him, all that my mother would say was that if I was very good, I might one day meet him. But I never did.

Being told to be *good* was also a puzzle, but in the end I began to see what they meant by it, and I was good. But often my idea of being good didn't coincide with theirs, and I would sit looking at them in complete bafflement while they, possibly taking my puzzlement for sulks, would chant infuriatingly:

> Cross-patch,
> Draw the latch,
> Sit by the fire and spin;
> Take a cup
> And sup it up
> Then have the neighbours in.

On the verge of tears—for I could never get angry, only tearful or bored—I would ask for:

> Knock at the door.
> Peep in,
> Lift the sneck,
> And walk in!

When she said " Knock at the door," my mother would

93

lightly knock on my forehead with the knuckles of her right hand. At " Peep in " (always a very protracted " ee " in " peep "), she would gently lift my eyelids. Then, to my constant astonishment, on " Lift the sneck " she would chuck me under the nose with her forefinger, and before I knew what had happened, I would feel her fingers, warm and work-roughened and smelling of new-baked bread, trampling on my tongue! It was a wonderful rhyme, full of physical surprises, for I could never remember the order of the actions. Everything astonished me with its familiar unexpectedness and whereas at the start of the rhyme I might have been silent with unshed tears, at the end I would be convulsed with laughter.

Another rhyme was sung by my father. Again I was certain that it was about a real person; everything he did was real, and slightly worrying:

> There was a man, he went mad,
> He jumped into a paper bag;
> The bag was too narrer,
> He jumped on a barrer,
> The barrer took fire,
> He jumped in a byre,
> The byre was all nasty,
> He jumped into a Cornish pasty;
> The pasty was full of meat,
> He jumped into Chester-le-Street;
> Chester-le-Street was full of stones,
> He fell down and broke his bones!

At the end of the rhyme, my father, holding my hands, would let me slide backwards down his outstretched legs, then would haul me up on his knees, and start all over again; I never got tired of this: I always liked things to be repeated again and again. I loved the sensation of falling, which made me howl with reckless merriment.

My mother, sitting knitting or sewing on her side of the fire, would be watching us with increasing disapproval.

" This'll end up in a crying match," she would say whenever I got over-excited. Then, as my father hauled me up for the final time, she would announce sharply and firmly:

" Now that's enough for to-night."

And to my father:

" You'll pull his arms out if you go on like this! " The awful picture evoked by these words always restored me to my usual quiet seriousness. I was so relieved to have both my arms in place! After that, I would go to bed like a good boy, but not before I had urged my mother to say:

> To bed, to bed,
> Sleepyhead,
> And up in the morning early!

If I was lucky I would be treated to a few more rhymes while I was being dressed for bed—*Wee Willie Winkie* or *Polly put the Kettle On*, or:

> Little Tommy Tacket
> Sits on his cracket.

The " cracket " was a part of every Tyneside home. It is a wooden stool, sometimes found with three legs, like a milking-stool, or more often, as ours was, oblong, heavy, with two solid pieces of wood at each end for legs. The cracket was my favourite fireside seat; it could be made into a boat when it was turned upside down. Right way up, with my legs astride, it would be a horse, and I would stump noisily round our kitchen floor on its back, crying " Gee-up, Neddy! " But it belonged to the kitchen: it was never allowed in the " room."

Finally, I will mention the rhyme I liked best of all; it is one that is very real to Tyneside children:

> Dance to your daddy,
> My little laddie,
> Dance to your daddy, my bonny lamb.
> And you shall have a fishie
> In a little dishie,
> You shall have a fishie when his boat comes in.

8. *Isa*

I WAS an only child, but not a lonely one. I was used to being on my own, and the idea that I might be lonely never entered my head. Then, as now, I was perfectly happy in my own company. Not that I lacked acquaintances: I responded always, I think, perfectly amiably to advances from animals, whom I liked best, and from human beings, whom I regarded with a certain amount of reserve. Strangers, wagging an arch finger at me, used to tell me I was a " bashful " boy—a word which I understood imperfectly in those days: I thought it had something to do with " bashing," which I knew all about, as ours was a violent neighbourhood. But I wasn't really " bashful "—all I wanted was to be left alone, and I was too polite to say so.

Sitting outside our front door, on the front step or in my pram, I was sometimes admired for my great mop of fair, almost-white, curly hair, and my big blue eyes that stared intently out of a very pale, chubby face. I was a very silent child, too, except when I was with people I knew very well. My mother tells me it used to " make her mad " to see me sitting solemnly without saying a word while other children of the same age " talked away twenty to the dozen." Kind strangers who stopped to chat could never get a word out of me: they would get their revenge by calling me " an old-fashioned bairn." But it meant nothing to me. I had nothing to say, and I distrusted baby-talk. Though the strange faces that occasionally peered round the hood of my pram at me aroused a kind of dispassionate interest—they usually belonged to old, black-shawled fisherwomen and pert little girls—I had no desire to enter into conversation with their owners, whom I observed with a non-committal detachment, as if they were curious objects whose unpredictable qualities needed long and patient study. But my philosophic silences, instead of discouraging the creatures, only seemed to provoke them to further useless conversational efforts. I was much more interested in my aunt's dog Rosie, the milkman's horse, the sparrows hopping in the gutter, the seagulls flying over the chimneys, and the cats that roamed up and down the street or lay sunning themselves on the hot flagstones of summer.

But when I reached the age of four, my circle of acquaintances began to widen, though I remained as reserved as ever. It was about this time that the first friend I ever knew entered my life. She was a little tomboy, slightly older than myself, a niece of Mrs. Battey who came to live with her for a while. Her name was Isa. What depths of innocent happiness I associate with that name! I can remember best of all her plump, bright-red cheeks, her black hair and dark eyes, the whiteness of her teeth when she gave her deep, hearty laugh, and her never-ending, boisterous good spirits. Without being at all " bossy," she had initiative and authority, and from the moment she set eyes on me, she took me firmly in hand. In appearance and character, there could hardly have been anyone more completely different from myself. Yet from our very first meeting, we were devoted to one another. My mother always kept me neat and clean, and my hair was always well brushed. From Isa I learnt first to appreciate " a sweet disorder in the dress": her black bob was always wind-blown; her bows and tortoiseshell hair-slides were always coming loose and her shoe-laces were never tied. There was a wonderful, wild freedom in all her speech and movements. She was energetic, practical, strong and gay: I was inclined to melancholy and reverie, and I did not have an abundance of animal spirits. But we adored one another, and were inseparable. Her nature, though rough and tempestuous, was warm and kind, and few people are able to resist warmth and kindness.

Isa was not more than a year older than myself, but to me she seemed an adult, though with none of the incomprehensible and tiresome ideas that most adults seemed to have. She was enterprising and dependable, and my mother soon entrusted me to her care. It was a wise and unselfish choice, for I obviously needed "taking out of myself," and Isa alone, as my mother saw at once, had the genius to do it. It was a perfect arrangement, and with Isa's devoted help I began to learn to face the world.

We would go rambling round the streets and back lanes of our immediate neighbourhood, walking happily hand-in-hand, and Isa would always be ready to defend me from big dogs and cruel boys and even crueller little girls. Seeing how devoted we were to one another, people would comment with what I seem to remember as unwilling surprise on our idyllic relationship. I recollect quite clearly how people used to say in our hearing that Isa should have been the boy, and that I should have been the girl, and indeed at the time I used to feel that it would have been much better so. I never minded what people said. I could always see *their* point of view, and was incapable of anger. If they thought that I should be a little girl, and Isa a little boy, then they could think so —it didn't matter to us.

A rhyme I learnt at this period seemed very puzzling:

> What are little boys made of?
> Slugs and snails
> And puppy-dogs tails,
> *That's* what little boys are made of!

" How unpleasant to be a little boy! " I would think. How much better to be a little girl, who is made of

> Sugar and spice,
> And all things nice!

And so—though I was in any case incapable of " taking offence "—I had no objections to being told that *I* should have been the little girl.

Isa's favourite rhyme, which she taught me, was:

> Boys and girls come out to play,
> The moon doth shine as bright as day,
> Come with a whoop,
> And come with a call,
> A halfpenny loaf will serve us all!

I was, I believe, shocked by this rhyme which seemed to celebrate the flouting of parental authority, and I firmly believed that after dark Isa came, "whooping and calling," along our street, and intrepidly scrambled " up the ladder and down the wall " while I was safely asleep in my bed.

I was filled with admiration for such daring, though I secretly disliked the idea of getting up in the middle of the night and running about the streets in my nightie, which was what the rhyme suggested. Sometimes, at twilight, she would come to our house, and press her nose against our front window while I was being dressed for bed, and call to my mother:

" Is Bimmy cummin' out a nigh'? "

In spite of her maturity, she still could not manage the " J " in " Jimmy," and spoke in a childish fashion that I found amusing; this was the only advantage I had over her, for I could speak " proper." But of course Isa was a law unto herself; she could stay out late at night and induce all the children in our street to come out and dance in the moonlight, while I slept safe in my warm little bed. I had no desire to join her midnight revels.

But it was right that Isa should do these things, for I recognised that she was " different": she was wild and anarchic, and none of the rules that applied to me applied to her devil-may-care existence. She would tuck her frock into her blue flannel bloomers, and " do the crab " or stand on her hands against the wall and pick her hanky off the ground with her teeth, or turn cartwheel after cartwheel while I stood primly and silently by, in an agony of delighted anxiety and adoration. She could talk, too, the hind leg off a donkey, with grown-ups as well as with her contemporaries. I could never have got a word in edgeways, even if I had wanted to. I remember the breathless silences of those days, when, with my hand in hers, I would be dragged speechlessly along while she kept up an incessant chatter about herself and the things we saw, and talked indefatigably to everyone we met, explaining who we were and where we came from and what we were doing, and interrupting her commentaries with great, deep hoots of laughter—and what a *deep* voice she had, like a boy's when it has broken.

Dear, childhood love, so pure, so unselfish—how true it was, and how happy! Yet we never thought of it as love, or as being in any way remarkable, despite the wondering exclamations of the grown-ups all around us. Sometimes Isa would take me on her knee, and " mother " me, but I don't ever remember any demonstrations of affection. We loved each other only as those love who do not know what love is, or what the world thinks it should be.

I liked Isa's independence and adventurousness, and I always trusted her implicitly, whatever she did and wherever she took me. She was brave, too. One day she came running into our front room from the street to tell my mother something and tripped on a " hooky " mat; she fell against the ornamental brass fender in front of the grate, cutting her forehead over the left eye. She bled profusely, yet she did not cry, and was very brave when she was taken away in an ambulance to the hospital to have the wound stitched. I was not present at the time of the accident, but when I was told about it later, I did not feel the slightest concern, because I felt that it was just the sort of thing that *would* happen to Isa, and I knew she was well able to cope with such eventualities. When she came back from hospital, she proudly displayed the marks of the stitches. She was marked for life: the accident left a semi-circular scar above her left eyebrow that gave her an even more rakish, devil-may-care look. The grown-ups tut-tutted over her, saying she " might have split her head open," or " put her eye out," but Isa, who, you must remember, was barely five, just laughed her deep, hoarse laugh and took me out to play. My father told her she looked like an old tom-cat after a fight, and that pleased her. With the bandage over her eye, she was irresistible. .

" Has 'e been bashin' ye aboot, hinney? " the neighbours asked her, pointing to me. We were looked upon as a future married couple, and we were perfectly happy to think of being married to one another, though marriage in our district did seem to consist of black eyes and beatings. I should have asked for nothing better than to be with Isa always: she was a wonderful girl—courageous, adroit, talkative and witty, and my boisterous cousins at Granny Johnson's thought the world of her, too, for she was one of their own kind.

        ★   ★   ★

I began to go on longer and longer expeditions with Isa, wandering round the grim, ugly streets with their odd names: Claypit Lane, Back Frederick Street, Ogle Terrace, George Potts Street, Laygate Lane, Commercial Road, Corstorphine Town, Candlish Street, Roman Road, Trajan Street, H. S. Edwards Street, the Mill Dam; we were not supposed to go to the latter, because it was considered dangerous—we might fall in the river. One of my great-uncles had been drowned there. And I hardly liked to mention the place, because " Dam " was a " bad word." There were long vistas of melancholy brick terrace houses, often with the huge wheels of pithead winding gear turning at the end of them. I liked watching the two great pithead wheels of St. Hilda's Colliery, just behind St. Hilda's Church in the Market Place. They were elegant wheels, thin-spoked and black against the grey northern skies; they revolved in opposite directions when a cage was being hauled to the surface, and this seemed to make them twinkle merrily, like a charming toy placed capriciously over the grim earth and the terrible coal-pits beneath.

Sometimes there would be discovered, at the end of a long street, a glimpse of the river, and North Shields on the opposite bank—ships' masts, smoking funnels, gliding flags and rigging—or a sudden startling view of the sea-horizon, stretched high and tight as an empty clothes-line between house and house. And along this high, sharp line, a ship would be creeping like a cut-out toy, her smoke-stack leaving a trail of brown smoke over the sky; or we would stand and watch the disappearing hull of a departing steamer, as she slowly dipped down out of sight over the edge of our world.

" It's going to Brazil, where the nuts come from," Isa would pronounce, and though I felt she was wrong, I would never contradict her.

I remember wandering with Isa under seemingly endless, towering blank brick walls that shut off colliery railways or the yards of works or docks. How long and high those windowless walls appeared to us, and how boring! Their blankness used to fill me with bleak anxiety.

" Are we *lost*? " I would suggest to Isa.

" Wey nor, man! " she would reply, hauling me along behind her. Often I think we *were* lost, but I trusted her to find the way home, and she always did. " Being lost " was one of my terrors, almost as bad as " being taken away by the gipsies." Those tall, dead walls that never seemed to lead anywhere used to induce a sense of panic in me. How wearisome it was, in summer, to have to walk along beside them—sometimes I felt as if it would take all afternoon to get to the end. My legs would grow tired, my feet would drag and stumble, but still Isa strode sturdily along, encouraging me, urging me to " pick my feet up," and even carrying me pick-a-back for a few yards. Just when things seemed to me at their blackest and gloomiest she would produce a sweet—a jelly-baby or a sherbet-dab, an aniseed ball or a piece of liquorice— and fortified and happy once again to be safe with such a generous provider, I would toddle on silently beside her chewing my sweet and listening spellbound to her animated chatter.

Once when we were walking past the long, drab brick wall of an Infirmary which Isa always called " the fever hospital " she commanded me to hold my breath until we had got past it, or else we would, so she hinted, " catch the fever." The ambulance, or " fever-van," was one of our nightmares, so I took a deep breath, and obediently held my nose, as she did. But as we walked along the endless wall, we began to find our breath giving out, so with agonised, speechless glances at one another, we started to run as fast as we could, holding our noses hard, and just as I felt my lungs were about to burst we reached the end of the infirmary wall and we were able to breathe safely again. It was the only occasion on which Isa was silent for any considerable length of time. She made up for it afterwards in sighs, laughs and panting exclamations, which I tried to copy, and nonstop chatter about the fever and how it turned you black all over. At that moment a Lascar seaman turned the corner on his way to join a ship at the Mill Dam, and Isa said:

" Look, Bimmy, 'e's got the fever, 'e's going black all over! "

The poor seaman rounded his eyes at our terrified faces, and we took to our heels again, never once looking back.

Another favourite excursion was to the " Coble Landing," which, if I recall it aright, was at the very end of that always endless-seeming, desolate street, Mile End Road. " Coble " is the Geordie word for a small rowing-boat, and I suppose the coble landing was where the fishermen and tugboat men and pilots landed their craft. I don't ever remember seeing anyone land there: all that remains in my memory is a long, steep flight of rickety, black, wet wooden steps that led down a precipitous bank to the river Tyne. As a child, I thought it a terrible drop —there was a rather loose wooden railing at the edge; but heights always filled me with a kind of happy terror, and I would rock on the wooden railing and imagine myself falling, falling, falling. . . . Beyond the landing lay the great, grey river, moving slowly down into the broad harbour, bearing coasters, pilot-craft, tugs, trawlers, dredgers, ferry boats, oil-tankers, and cargo ships and occasionally mournfully-hooting liners from Scandinavia. Forests of scaffolding and masts rose from the shipyards, where even in daytime you could catch sight of the blue spark of a far-off acetylene burner used by an unseen welder or riveter. Those flashes were our kingfishers. It was the same sort of blue flash as that made by our tram-trolleys.

Then we would have pin-flattening expeditions. We would " pinch " a few pins from home—heaven only knows what my father's great-aunt would have had to say about that—lay them on the tram lines and wait for a tram to roll over them. As soon as the tram had passed, we would rush out into the road and, if we were lucky, we would find a perfectly-flattened pin, still quite warm from the friction of the tram's iron wheels. Sometimes, when we were " flush " and had a farthing or a ha'penny to spare, we would put the coin on the tram line and when we had retrieved it, it would be wafer-thin, with all the lettering gone and the king's head very squashed. We knew all the trams by sight: each had a different personality. We were very impressed by new ones, which were smartly-painted and had imposing names painted on their flanks—*Monarch of Bermuda* was the name of one, I remember, and I felt especially possessive about that one because my own Uncle Jack lived in Bermuda. But these belonged to later years.

In those days, we never bothered about the dangers of traffic. We used to run blithely along the tram lines; no one ever told us not to, and we were never " run over," though we once got rather panicky about a runaway horse and cart that came careering down Robertson Street; the horse's hoofs were clashing against the cobblestones, making showers of sparks, and the cart was banging madly from side to side behind it. I got a quick glimpse of one of the horse's eyes behind its " blinker "—the eye was huge, shining, dark, with long, fine eyelashes; there was a lot of bloodshot white in the pupil, and the foam was flying from its yellow teeth. The metal bit was dangling and the mane was foam-flecked. The horse made an awful, slithering clatter over the wet cobbles, then the cart overturned and brought the horse down a few feet from where I stood shaking in Isa's arms. I heard sharp cracks as the horse's front legs broke, then Isa hid my face, but she went on looking. The horse was shot, though we did not stay to see that. All I remember is how terrible it was to see the horse struggling helplessly on the cobbles, lifting its head in vain, and whinnying and

screaming. It reminded me of another shocking nursery
rhyme I knew:

> I had a little pony,
>> His name was Dapple Grey,
> I lent him to a lady
>> To ride a mile away.

> She whipped him, she lashed him,
>> She drove him through the mire;
> I wouldn't lend my pony now
>> For that bad lady's hire.

I couldn't eat or sleep for days after that accident. It
had shown me what suffering is. Ever after that I loved
horses above all other animals, and I couldn't bear to see
them being whipped or dragging great loads of coal, with
the driver sitting on the shafts.

" They don't feel anything, son," my father and mother
would say, to console me when I came in crying after
seeing horses cruelly handled. But I knew they were just
saying that to comfort me. I had begun to be familiar
with the world of pain.

9. Infant Joys

THE OCCASIONS when we could afford to put a ha'penny on the tram lines were very rare, for in those days a ha'penny could buy two aniseed balls, our favourite sweet. They were delicious, I'm sure, but I seem to remember they were boring after the first roughness had worn off, and we had to suck loud and long until the little seed at the centre was reached. Isa told me that if we ate too many of them we would fall asleep and never wake up, so we were careful never to have more than two in our mouths at once.

For a ha'penny, too, we could buy a pipe made of liquorice, its " bowl " sprinkled with bright red hundreds-and-thousands to represent fire. We could get a packet of five pink-tipped sugar cigarettes, but these always seemed to us rather poor value for money—they didn't last long enough. A ha'penny would also buy a drum of " Cut Cavendish," or a gobstopper or a portion of cinder toffee. We were passionately fond of that golden, sticky, crunchy sweetmeat, with its slightly burnt flavour, in its white wrapper, from which every precious crumb had to be licked before it was thrown away. And we often bought " Dolly " Mixture, with its rare, red, breath-scenting

" cachoos." I seem to remember, too, from this period —just before I started going to the Infants' School— delicacies such as toffee-apples, " Mixed Shot," liquorice " bootlaces," the wrapped lumps in the blue-and-white tins of Farrar's Original Harrogate Toffee, bubble gum, Berwick Cockles, Edinburgh Rock, glacier mints and liquorice " allsorts." There were, too, those milk-tray caramels that seemed so enormous and so hard when I put one in my mouth—it filled me with blissful despair, for I could hardly get my jaws working on it at first. They were so big and unmanageable, I used to think I would never get them under control, and when I did finally manage to dispose of one, my jaws would ache and throb with the exertion. They needed really concentrated work.

Another treat was Sherbet Dabs: we got a caramel-flavoured lollipop which we dipped into a bag of sherbet. A similar " good ha'porth " was the Soda Fountain, a cylinder full of sherbet that had to be sucked up through a tube of liquorice. Two little sweet " cakes," spongy, tasteless, pale-yellow in colour, and with fluted edges, were provided " free " with every Soda Fountain. Sucking up that sherbet was quite a business, especially if it was rather damp, and there were blockages in the slowly-disintegrating liquorice tube.

Toffee-apples were a special delight. They were usually homemade, and would be displayed in a tray in the front window of someone's " room." The combination of flavours—the sticky burnt caramel of the toffee with its crisp, flat " crown," and the sharp, sweet sourness of the half-green apple—was unforgettable.

My mother did not like me to have chewing-gum which she told me was made from old candle-ends. But

Isa would sometimes give me a piece. I was repeatedly warned that if I was given a piece of chewing-gum, I was not to swallow it, for if I did, it would tie itself into knots in my inside. Once I did swallow a piece which Isa had given me. We didn't dare tell my mother, and we lived in terror for several days; then I think we just forgot all about it. I never really liked chewing-gum; it was very insipid after the first fine rush of peppermint had died away, and when I pulled it out in long, fine strings from my mouth, I got it all over my hair and face and clothes. I preferred eating a watch made of pink-and-white sugar, or a slab of " wigga-wagga " toffee.

We used to buy transfers, too—" Billy Stampers," as the children on Tyneside call them. We could get a whole sheet for a ha'penny: we thought butterflies and birds and pretty little girls were rather " cissy," so we always bought transfers in the form of a strip cartoon, telling us the adventures of Felix the wonderful cat; there was a song about him that was all the rage:

> Felix kept on walking, kept on walking still,
> With his hands behind him
> You will always find him. . . .

These " Billy Stampers " were printed in a revolting shade of yellow ochre, and black. We did not " stamp " them into books, but on to our own persons. After tearing one carefully from the sheet, we would breathe noisily upon the printed surface, apply it to the back of the hand, the wrist, the knee, the arm, or any available patch of bare flesh, then cover it generously with " spit." Then followed the most important part of the operation, without which it could not possibly succeed: the incantation. To

the tune of *Pat-a-cake, pat-a-cake, baker's man,* we would
chant these words:

> Billy Billy Stamper,
> Stamp my hand,
> Stamp my hand
> As hard as you can.
>
> Billy Billy Stamper,
> Clag to my hand,
> Clag to my hand
> As fast as you can.

While we were chanting this, we would be belabouring
the back of the transfer with our fists. Then came the
anxious moment when the paper was gently peeled off,
discovering the glossy yellow-and-black illustration to yet
another of Felix's adventures. Sometimes I would transfer
a whole story to my bare arm or leg. I once had two
butterflies imprinted on my behind. They were very
difficult to get off.

★   ★   ★

Sometimes Isa and I would be allowed, after prolonged
entreaty, to " make a tent " in the backyard. We would
fix a clothes-horse or a few broken clothes-props between
the rain-water tubs and the wall, and drape any old things
we could induce my mother or Mrs. Battey to lend us
over this framework—old bedspreads, mats or curtains
were the most sought-after materials. Then we would lay
an old " hooky " mat and cushions inside. If we were
very lucky, and the weather was fine, we would be
allowed to have tea in our tent, and to play houses with
the fireside things—the tongs, the little brush, the shovel

and the ash-rake. Those were grand, serious occasions, when we sat on old cushions in the dust-smelling semi-gloom of our gipsy dwelling, and ate warm, freshly-baked " oven-bottom cake " covered with melting butter, and drank mugs of hot, strong, sweet tea made in a doll's tea-pot. Isa, of course, supervised everything, and kept it all shipshape. But in the end, however hard we tried to improve our retreat, it would fall down round our ears, and we would struggle, laughing and tousled, out of the engulfing billows of material. Often one of us might get a nasty knock on the head from one of the falling props, but we did not care: we had learned not to cry at such mishaps, but to look upon them as great jokes. Sometimes, if I had been really hurt, I would find myself on the verge of tears, but then Isa would pull such comical faces and say such amusing things that I had to laugh in spite of the pain, and was spared the dreadful ignominy of bursting into tears.

When it was sunny and there was not too much wind, we would drag a clothes-horse and a few tattered curtains up to the Lawe, a stretch of grass on a cliff above the North Marine Park, overlooking the sea. It was only a few minutes' walk from our house, beyond the Roman Remains at the top of Robertson Street, but it seemed to take ages to get there, for we would be heavily laden and excitement made us impatient. Struggling along with our sticks and bundles, it was always a grand moment when we glimpsed " The Fort," which was the name we gave to a large, concrete, battlemented house by the gates to the Lawe: it was a rather mysterious house, with very tiny windows, surrounded by dense shrubbery, and no one was ever seen to enter or leave it. Isa said it was full of spies.

The Only Child

We would carefully select a spot that seemed clean and thickly-turfed, and we would set to work putting up our tent. There would sometimes be battles with gangs of boys and girls. We were always in the minority, for we never went about with other children. Isa would fight like a fury to defend her rights; I'm afraid I just used to stand by rather helplessly, or even run away. Isa never minded. She knew I didn't like fighting, and that I hated to inflict pain on anyone. I would stand aghast watching her biting and kicking and pulling hair as well as any lad from the " low streets." Then, if I had not run away, we would return home, our arms round each other's necks, dishevelled, dirty, and bloody. But we didn't care about scraped knees and torn hair and bleeding noses. The only really awful thing was when our clothes got ripped, or when we lost a part of the tent. Then we knew we were " in for it." But as long as we did not lose the clothes-horse, no one really minded if we came home without a dirty old piece of cloth.

We knew, too, the illicit joy of spending our Sunday school collection money on " tiger-nuts " and coconut ice. The sweets used to taste like dust in our mouths; we knew we were " doing wrong," and we never enjoyed them, for we had to gobble them up quickly before we got to the red-brick chapel at the top of Robertson Street; it was, I think, a Methodist chapel, and I believe I was baptised there. I don't recall anything at all about the Sunday school, though I have faint memories of tea parties being held there at which I was unwillingly present. Eventually we salved our consciences by deciding to use only half our collection money for the purchase of sweets; now we could enjoy the virtuous bliss of self-denial and relish our forbidden sweets as well. But it still worried me, and a few years later, when I was struck by lightning, I believed it was the wrath of God manifesting itself because I had not offered up my mite to Him.

Going for a walk in the park was another wild adventure. South Shields has magnificent parks; the two near the sea—the South Marine and the North Marine Parks—were our favourites, though we also liked to go for walks in the cemeteries, where the glass-globed china flowers fascinated us and we played at houses among the tombstones, or in the Roman Remains, a rather drably-preserved Roman ruin from which our town derived its motor-registration letters—CU, standing for Caer Urfa.

The North Marine Park had a dilapidated aviary in which lived two storks and a few small birds: it was a sad place, all rusted chicken wire and shrubbery. But there was also a grand flight of stone steps which had a smooth brick balustrade down which we liked to slide. There were enormous rockeries, one of which contained a tunnel through which we could actually walk. The curved backs of the park benches were grand for sliding on, too: the iron, green-painted arm-rests at each end depicted squirrels and leaves. It was pleasant, at the bowling-green, to watch the " woods " gliding over the unbelievably smooth turf; I used to like to watch the white disc on the side of the bowls spinning wildly at first, and then settling down to a still centre, and the gentle clatter of the bowls as they were knocked back into the ditch by the players' feet was like music. There were enormous flower-beds blazing with gaudy colour—long striped borders of pansies and great clumps of dahlias and asters—and there were lawns that seemed to stretch to infinity. Some of my first reading lessons took place in the parks, where I used to stand on a bench reading the

The Only Child

" Bye-Laws governing the provision of Public Parks," and vaguely understood that there were many things which were " not done " in a public pleasure-ground. I believe there was one clause which said something to the effect that "undesirable persons were not admitted," and we were sure that this meant Isa and myself. We were always walking on the grass, in spite of the little notices saying " Keep off the Grass "; it gave us a naughty little thrill to run along the edges of the lawns. Then a cry would go up from Isa:

" Parky! There's the parky! "

The park-keeper was like a policeman, but he couldn't run as fast as we did. We lived in mortal terror of being caught by the parky and locked up in the aviary all night, which was what he threatened us with. Yet whenever I was walking in the park with my mother, he would say nothing; but children hated and feared him.

The South Marine Park was even better than the North Marine Park, whose name seemed to cast a certain chill over it. In the South Marine Park there was the lake, and the swans, and a bandstand. The bandstand was a fine affair, I thought, with lots of lacy ironwork and a marvellous fretted cupola that looked like the top of our silver sugar-dredger at home. My mother loved listening to the military bands that played there, and she told me that before I was born she used to go there every afternoon to listen to the band, so that when I grew up I should love music. Her far-sighted plan was certainly successful, for I always loved music from my earliest days. On sunny afternoons, we would go and sit on a bench near the band-stand, or, if we had a little money to spare, we would hire an uncomfortable folding-chair in the grass-stepped enclosure and listen to *Poet and Peasant* overture or the *William Tell* overture and Gilbert and Sullivan and German and Strauss and Meyerbeer. They would be played by military bands, and colliery bands—the Boldon Colliery Brass Band was one of the best in the country. It was fine to see the sunlight glinting on the brass and silver instruments, and to listen to a melting cornet solo, or a virtuoso piece on the trumpet or clarinet. I knew the names of all the instruments before I was five, and could identify them by the sounds they made—flute, piccolo, fife, trombone, bassoon, tuba, horn and clarinet. It was lovely, too, to wander under the cool trees by the lake and listen to the strains of a lavish waltz swirling faintly through the rhododendrons and mingling with the cries of children and the cries of gulls, while the lake-water glittered in the sun, and the sea-breeze whitened the leaves and stirred the sweet-smelling flowering privets. It was thrilling to enter the park gates, with their banner advertising the performances of a visiting band, and throw our entrance money— Silver Collection!—into the sheet stretched out at the entrance, while the music of the opening number sounded through the rustling willows and the flowering hawthorns and the " hush-hush " of feet hurrying towards the bandstand along the sand-strewn alleys. But at evening, when the fairy lights were switched on round the musicians, I felt a sad edge on my happiness. Oh, those faintly-chiming town clocks, that, with the growing murmur of the sea, accompanied the nostalgic waltzes of my mother's girlhood and made my heart ache for her, and for the passing of time: *Nights of Gladness, Sobre las Olas, Blue Danube, Gold and Silver*—what power you have to charm, and haunt, and hurt! They were all laughter, gaiety, remorse, regret, those tunes, and my heart was always filled with a bittersweet pang when I heard my mother faintly humming them, a lost smile on her lips, her neat little dancer's foot beating time to *The Barcarolle* from the *Tales of Hoffman*, or the waltz from the *Belle of New York*. The Boldon Colliery Band, and my mother's abstracted smile, taught my infant innocence more about life than anything ever since.

But on summer mornings, when the band was not playing, it was the lake that Isa and I rushed to. We could see the water sparkling through the iron railings and the privet hedges and the trunks of trees as we ran along the street to the entrance to the park. There were never many people about in the mornings. If our luck was in, there might be a model yacht enthusiast sailing his model yacht from one side of the lake to the other, and we would watch him changing his rig and run round the lake with him to catch the yacht with a long rubber-tipped pole as it reached the opposite bank. There were model motor-boats, too, which spat and roared and smelt of methylated spirits. But best of all were the ducks standing on their heads in the water and shaking their tails, and the swans—snow-white, regal, orange-beaked, wary-eyed yet completely imperturbable. They snapped in a dignified manner at the bits of dry biscuit we brought them; the ducks pounced on the bread and the sparrows hopped beside us picking up the crumbs. There was an island in the centre of the lake; it concealed the swannery and the nesting places for the ducks among its stunted trees. We longed to live on that island, and planned how we would survive.

" We could live on fish from the lake," I suggested, rather dubiously.

" An' hev the parky after we? " exclaimed Isa.

" We could take the ducks' eggs."

"They're poison!" she vehemently replied. "Divven't let me ever see ye eating a duck's egg, or Aa'll bray ye."

But there was no way of getting to the island. The parky only used his boat to release yachts that had got stuck on its banks, and he would never allow us to go with him.

We loved the lake; it was better than the sea, for the sea was "ordinary." The lake was something special. We caught tiddlers in it, and took them home in jam jars. The cobbled sides were treacherous, and once I leaned over too far, and fell in. Isa hauled me out and dried my wet pants on a rose bush while I hid in the sea-smelling gentlemen's lavatory. Isa was a great one for the proprieties.

10. Shades of the Prison House

I HAD reached the age of five, and it was time to start going to school. Already I knew my letters, could count up to twenty, and could recite many rhymes and sing a few songs. I could deliver these in a broad Tyneside accent; but I would sing them only to my mother and father and Isa. From my mother I had inherited a passionate love of music, a strong rhythmical sense and a gift for mimicry. I would stand on our kitchen table, taking care not to knock the gas mantle, and sing in the hoarse, drunken Geordie voice of a collier on a Saturday night:

She's a big lass and a bonny lass and she likes hor beor,
An' they caal hor Cushie Butterfield, an' Aa wish she
    wore heor!

Or:

    Wheer ha' *ye* been aal the day,
      Billy Boy, Billy Boy,
    Wheer ha' *ye* been aal the day me Billy Boy?

I could also sing *The Keel Row* and accompany it with a comic dance; *Blaydon Races* and *Caller Herrin'* were of course also in my repertoire. Best of all I liked to sing:

> The bonny pit laddie, the canny pit laddie,
> The bonny pit laddy for me, O!
> He sits in a hole as black as the coal,
> And gets the bright siller for me, O.

> The bonny pit laddie, the canny pit laddie,
> The bonny pit laddie for me, O!
> He sits on his cracket and brings home his packet,
> And brings the bright siller to me, O!

But when I started school, my singing and dancing days came to an end. For though I could sing and dance quite happily in front of my mother and father and Isa, in public I was afflicted with misery and could never say a word to strangers. It was a sad day for me, and for my dear mother, when she took me up Robertson Street, past the red-brick chapel, to the gates of Baring Street Infants' School and parted from me there. I walked with shaking knees into the milling playground, looking back often at my mother who stood waving and bravely smiling beyond the gates. She told me, long afterwards, how lonely that first morning had seemed, when I went to school for the first time.

Isa was not at school with me. Being slightly older, she had started school some time before; I believe she attended a school in a different part of the town. I do not remember much of that first day at school, apart from the chill struck at my heart by the big, gloomy central hall with its large rocking-boat and rocking-horse that we were never allowed to play on. I vaguely remember my first teacher—a bosomy, red-haired lady with protruding teeth and a jolly face. She frightened me. Her voice was so shockingly loud and clear and brisk, after the playful gentleness of my mother's, and she had no trace of Geordie accent. She spoke in such a refined voice that for several days, until I got used to it, I couldn't understand what she was saying. I think we spent the first morning just sitting in our desks, listening to the mistress read, and learning to put our hands up and say, " Please, miss."

I wore a new woollen guernsey—" gansey " is the name given to it on Tyneside—which buttoned on the shoulder with three mother-of-pearl buttons. My mother had knitted it for me. It reminded me of her, and as I sat in that hideous classroom I felt the contrast between the love of home and the indifference of school so strongly that I had great difficulty in restraining my tears. No one had told me about the lavatory, and I remember looking down at the floor and being astonished to see it all wet under my feet; a little boy sitting next to me jumped up and shouted:

" Please, miss, 'e's wet the floor! "

I don't know how I got through that morning. At dinner-time my mother came to fetch me home. I was in disgrace with the teacher, but not, I was glad to find, with my mother.

" She should have told you where to go," my mother said when I had explained what had happened.

She had nothing but scorn for our teachers, whom she said were incompetent and unfit to have charge of little children.

" You'd think they'd never been kids themselves," she said indignantly. " They want to use a little common sense. If they'd had children of their own . . ." And here her natural goodness asserted itself. " Poor things, nobody would ever want to marry *them*! "

I wept all dinner-time, and did not want to go back in the afternoon. But my mother, though tender, was firm, and back I went in a dry pair of pants, and found things weren't so bad after all. We were given strips of coloured paper to weave into mats, and later we made chains with loops of shiny coloured gummed paper—I can still taste that gum on my tongue: I licked so many pieces of paper that my mouth went dry.

It was a fine, long chain I made, and I was very proud of it. At the end of school I ran out into the school yard with my chain fluttering gaily behind me. I wanted to get home as quickly as possible to show it to my mother and father. But just as I was running through the iron gates out into the street, one of the " big girls " spitefully snapped it. I was bewildered. It was my first encounter with real malignity. All I could do was to stare at her in amazement.

" Whe d'ye think ye're lukkin' at? " she snarled.

I couldn't answer. I could only stand and wonder at the useless thing she had done, and look in despair at my broken chain.

" Garn! " she said, showing her teeth. I fled.

Only one of the links was broken. Perhaps I could mend it at home. But however hard I tried, that link refused to be mended. All the glue had been licked off. I stuck it with lashings of spit—no good. I tried flour-paste and condensed milk, but always the sodden paper tore or came apart. I was in despair. It was dreadful to think that the most beautiful thing I had ever made was broken, and could not be mended.

Day followed day at school, and I became more and

123

more unhappy: I felt out of place. I used to long for the end of the afternoon, when we would be bidden to fold our hands in our laps, and sing:

> Now the day is over,
> Night is drawing nigh,
> Shadows of the evening
> Steal across the sky. . . .

That sad little tune, with its haunting simplicity, would move me every time I heard it. As I sat, feeling very small and lonely, in the falling dusk of the schoolroom, and looked out of the high windows at the northern evening sky, my heart would ache with the poignancy of the words, and once again I would catch fleeting glimpses of the spirit-world, and knew better than ever what ghosts and dying meant. I can still hear those sharp infant voices singing, so sweetly, " the evening," and " steal."

Darkness. Ugliness. Those are the things I remember from my infant school days. The school was built of dirty brick. The drab playground, without a single bush or tree, was made of asphalt, and it was surrounded by blank brick walls. Iron railings shut off a basement where coke was kept for the boilers. Sometimes when we came to school in the morning there would be a great pile of coke by the basement railings, and the bigger boys and girls would start jumping about on it, and a fine grey dust would rise from their revels. Then the school caretaker, a sad little man who always appeared in shirt-sleeves, wearing a greenish bowler hat, would shout up from the basement steps, threatening to take them to the head-mistress for " a dose of the strap." He had a thin, complaining, ineffective voice; the boys and girls would

run away in gleeful terror; they knew he never carried
out his threats.

The classrooms were dull. They smelt of sand, dis-
infectant and chalky blackboard dusters. There was a
sour chill in the cloakrooms. The walls of some of the
classrooms were made of varnished partitions through
which you could hear the class next door stodging through
the alphabet or the Lord's Prayer or *Thirty Days hath
September*. On the walls hung religious pictures, maps of
the Empire, photographs from *Child Education*, a large
calendar and the alphabet. On the window-sills were
bulb vases of dark green glass, and a saucer or two with
carrot-tops growing in them. There was nothing of the
gaiety and freedom and liveliness of an infant's class to-
day; but I think the class as a whole was a happy one, for
we liked our jolly teacher, though I don't believe she
taught us very much. I learned to write, painfully
gripping the thin ribbed shank of a new school pen, by
copying out dozens of times set phrases like " Virtue is
its own Reward." Those capital Rs were a trial. I
remember the funny little exercise books we had to do
our writing in, with two very widely-spaced lines to every
small page: it was the devil of a job to hold it down,
when your steel nib was pressing and pricking the paper.
The teacher would walk round, her fat arms comfortably
folded over her bust, and tell us to make all our letters
slope the same way. This was something I could never
do, and it always amazed me, when she extended my
down and up strokes with her blue pencil, to see how far
from parallel they were. I thought she went out of her
way to make my handwriting look worse than it really was.

In class, I was very slow, untidy and silent. I trembled
with apprehension nearly all the time. Sums were a

mystery to me: I just couldn't add or multiply. The squared paper on which we did sums still makes me unhappy whenever I use it. Reading lessons were a little better, because I didn't mind books. ~~When I first~~ started school, I was able to read fairly well, but there were occasional words that baffled me and held me up. After a few weeks of patient struggling, a dam seemed to burst inside my head: I heard myself reading big words aloud, without much hesitation, and soon I found I could read fluently. The last word to puzzle me was " laugh." I remember poring over this odd word in my reader. The sentence ran: " And so the princess began to laugh and laugh and laugh." What *could* it be that the princess had begun to do? I was reading aloud, the class listening hard to catch my words, for I had a very soft voice. I came to the first " laugh," got my tongue round the " l," voiced the " a," and—it was like a miracle!—the " f " sound followed as if instinctively. " *Laugh!* " I said, very slowly. As the other two " laughs " came with increasing confidence, I really felt like laughing myself, for the first time since I had started school. But I could not imagine why on earth " augh " should spell " aff." I was glad to have mastered the awkward word. Flushed by success, I uttered the first sentence I had ever spontaneously spoken in class:

" Please, miss, doesn't that word *look* as if it's laughing?"

And indeed, those two vowels in the middle of the word looked to me like the open mouth of someone laughing. The other members of the class thought I was " daft." The teacher, too, seemed rather taken aback by my question: she was quite a nice woman, but she obviously hadn't looked at the word in that light before.

" Yes, doesn't it? " she replied after a discernible

pause, vaguely smiling, narrowing her eyes and putting rather too much " gush " into her words. I could see she didn't really understand what I meant. Yet I knew I was right, and that she was a booby, and I had one of the few moments of true happiness I ever knew in that school.

Then I asked her why, when the word was written l-a-u-g-h, it was pronounced l-a-f-f.

" Now you little people don't need to worry your heads about that," she said, and told us to shut our readers. She always called us " You little people," and I rather liked it. I had no desire to be big: it was enough, for the moment, to be one of the " little people." As long as we were " little people," I felt I could cope with things.

Friday afternoons were the best times at school. We were allowed to bring our own books to read, during the last half of the afternoon. In the first half, the girls did knitting and sewing. The boys had to do clay modelling with dirty, dark-green, boring, smelly clay. We would much rather have knitted. I used to make little men out of the clay—how it stuck under the finger-nails!—like the ones I made with dough and currants on baking day at home. We were not encouraged to make interesting things with the clay, and most of the boys copied me, making shapeless men. One boy did a lady, and he was sharply reprimanded: he had to squash her up at once. The remaining boys made battleships, which I hated: they looked so tedious, so unfloatable. I was quite unable to work up any excitement about mechanical things: tram cars were the only things I really liked, but when I asked the teacher if I could make one with my clay she said: " Now, then, don't be silly." So I made a model of teacher: when she saw it she said it was very nice. But when I told her it was meant to be *her*, she said it was nasty and told me to squash it up and do a tram car if I wished. Oh, the boredom of those Friday afternoon clay-modelling classes! It was a relief to get my nose into a nice book after playtime.

We had one wonderful " art " lesson, in which I learned to mix colours. We were given an oblong piece of white cartridge paper and a piece of red pastel. We had to lay the colour on very heavily at one end of the oblong, then use it more and more sparingly until, when we got to the other end, the paper was still more or less white. Then—oh, mystery!—we were given a piece of yellow pastel, and told to use it as we had used the red, but starting at the opposite end of the oblong. I shall never forget my amazed delight when I found myself creating a new colour—*orange*. My excitement increased when I found that red and blue made purple, and blue and yellow made green. Then we were told all about the spectrum, and about primary and secondary colours, and in the next art lesson I made a very smudgy spectrum. To-day, this would not be considered a very "imaginative" way to teach children about colour, but I found every minute of those lessons entrancing, and I have remembered them to this day. They were factual: they gave information; and that was what I wanted. The youngest children, just as much as older ones, need facts rather than " imagination " from their teacher. They already have a large natural supply of imagination which needs no stimulation. Out of the bare facts of those art lessons, something magical came to light.

*   *   *

I did not make friends. My silence and reserve caused

other children—and some of my teachers—to treat me as if I were an idiot. They called me a " loony," but I did not mind. I detested the playtimes, for I did not like games of any kind. The playground, filled with a swarm of shrieking, violent children was a place of terror to me. I would try to make myself as inconspicuous as possible in the semi-darkness of the " shed," a large open shelter at one end of the playground. On rainy days, this was the only place where the whole school could shelter from the rain during playtime. For me, rain came to mean nightmares of cross, rough, bullying, ugly children kicking and punching and stealing one's possessions. My mother usually gave me an apple or an orange for playtime, but this was generally snatched from me before I had time to eat it. That part of school life was utter misery. To-day, whenever I smell orange peel, I remember the terror I felt at playtimes.

There were large rubbish bins of green-painted wood in the shed, and in these we put our sandwich papers and used paper bags and apple cores—" gowks," we called them—and orange peel and banana skins. I used to stand every playtime beside one of these bins, shaking with fright, and smelling the stale stench of orange peel and paper that rose from it. I was once stuffed into a rubbish bin by a crowd of big boys. I thought I was going to suffocate. I couldn't get out. The whole school stood round, jeering and laughing, and no one offered to help me out. I thought of Isa, and refused to cry. The bell for lessons rang, but I was stuck fast in the bin, and the classes went in without me. I was so thankful to be left alone! It was a relief to be quiet. How strange the empty playground seemed; there were faint noises coming from the classroom windows—dreary chantings of multiplication tables and verses from the Bible. I made no further attempts to extricate myself, but crouched among the rubbish, the orange peel and the slimy banana skins. After what seemed a very long time the teacher came and hauled me out. She was very cross with me, and gave me a good shaking as she hurried me across the yard.

It was an unpleasant experience: I had been cowed and frightened, and made to feel that I was an outcast. It taught me to see the world outside my home as a barbaric and unfriendly place. But I also learned what the hunted fox must feel, and the flogged horse. A lonely child, I learned more and more to prefer my own company to that of other children.

My mother and father gave me what help and comfort they could: they knew how wretched I was, and sympathised, but they were firm with me too. I had to learn the hard way. But I could not explain to them just how terrible an agony that school was to me, for in those days I did not understand it myself. I was hurt and lost, and didn't know why. It is only now, looking back on those days, that I can realise what I suffered: I can see it all with detachment and even with humour. Perhaps, when we die, that is how we will look back on life—as a long school day, full of trials whose purpose and meaning we were ignorant of as long as we were alive, but that the growing-up of death allows us to look back on with detachment, and charity.

11. *Home Comforts*

THE TRYING times I had at the Infants' School made me love my home and my mother and father more than ever. I don't think I actually loved them *more*—that was not possible, and in any case " love " signified nothing then— but I began to realise how much they meant to me, how sad it was to be separated from them, even for a few hours a day, and how awful it would be, in this terrible new world of school and violence, if they were not there at all.

Coupled with my anxieties at school was the fear that, when I returned home at dinner-time or tea-time I should find them gone, the house locked up and deserted, or, even worse, occupied by strangers who would insist on adopting me as their son. So immediately after lessons were over, I would not linger in the classroom " sucking up to teacher " as the " teacher's pets " did; nor would I play in the school yard with top and whip or bat and ball as so many children did. I would take to my heels and run home as fast as I could. Sometimes the older children, seeing how eager I was to get home, would ambush me outside the school gates and keep me prisoner for five or ten minutes. I learned to submit without a struggle: there was no point in offering any resistance.

The Only Child

I had discovered that when I didn't put up a struggle my tormentors soon got bored, and let me go: but if I started biting and kicking, that always aroused their basest instincts, and they would bait me unmercifully, calling: " Kicky donkey! Kicky donkey!" I had no scruples, when I *did* resist, about the methods I used.

I very soon began to see that I had a temper after all, a real Irish " paddy " which probably was a legacy from the Irish ancestors on my mother's side who lived in County Mayo. When, after never knowing what anger was, I suddenly felt myself possessed by a fury—a cold rage that surprised me with the strength and determination of its expression—I was shocked and not a little frightened. Rage made me without warning tremble and grow cold: it revealed the presence of a stranger within me. I would feel the blood draining away from my face, and a damp chill coming over my clenched hands. Instinctively I disliked and distrusted this terrifying sensation, and it very rarely overcame my natural meekness. I think the other children were afraid of its manifestations, too, for it brought with it a dreadful violence, always hideous, always unexpected. Yet as soon as it had passed, I forgot about it altogether. The other children were afraid of my passion, yet time and time again they tried to provoke it. I found that as soon as they realised I was not going to " get in a paddy," they left me alone. It was an admirable training in non-resistance and self-control. Eventually, after months of torture, my tormentors turned their attentions to more satisfying victims—children who howled and screamed and wept.

If I ran all the way, I could be home in two minutes, and I would arrive at the back door panting and happy.

Home Comforts

My mother always had dinner ready for me, and it was a sad dinner-time for me when there was no rice pudding, my favourite dish. On cold, winter days we would have our dinner on trays by the fireside, while the wind roared outside and rain lashed the window-panes and the sea boomed beyond the house-tops. They were happy, cosy, intimate meals. It was a great treat to have dinner or tea by the blazing fire, with our feet up on the sparkling brass fender of the whitewashed hearth. But it made going back to school even harder. If there was dense fog outside, I would sit by the fire in my slippers until the last possible minute, listening to the glum blasts of the foghorn and the wailing sirens of fog-bound ships outside the harbour. Then, with a high-pitched urgency, the school bell would begin to ring, and I would scramble into my coat and cap and outdoor shoes, cover my mouth and nose with my muffler, and dash out into the dead, damp fog. The school bell, rung by the old caretaker in his shirt-sleeves and bowler hat, filled me with anguish and excitement, and as I ran along, carefully avoiding the black cracks in the pavement, my steps kept time—*had* to keep time with it. These were two magical devices I had invented to keep trouble away. Another was to cross the toecap of my shoe with spit whenever I saw a white horse. Picking up coal was also lucky, and it was advisable to cross one's fingers if a black cat ran across one's path.

One morning I was in such a hurry to get to school— I had left it rather late, and the bell was ringing maddeningly, as if it knew I was in a fix—my mother put my shoes on the wrong feet while I was struggling into my coat. All morning my feet felt uncomfortable, but I did not realise what was wrong until I got home for dinner and told my mother how my feet hurt. She told me she'd put my shoes on the wrong feet, and we had a good laugh. But it was the first time I'd ever known her make a mistake, and there was an undercurrent of uncertainty in my laughter.

Yes, it was wonderful to be at home, and not at school, and whenever I was in the house I would look at things with an intent, almost morbid thoroughness, as if I might never see them again. The patterns on the tablecloths, the plates, the wallpaper, the linoleum and on our big Axminster carpet in the front room—how proud my mother was of it, and looked after it so well that as I write now, my feet still rest on its almost undimmed, magical splendour—all these I studied with obsessional intensity until I knew every colour, every repetition, every convolution of their extraordinary designs. The carpet was the most interesting of all. It had all kinds of peculiar abstract shapes woven into it, and I would try hard to rationalise them: one was a tram car, several of them were cakes or sweets, one was a tortoise, another a castle, another a giant beetle. I spent hours poring over those patterns, trying to extract the hidden meaning which I was sure lay behind them. But they were very mysterious —even my mother and father couldn't tell me what they meant.

I would stare and stare at the white, set face of a travelling clock in a green leather folding case which stood, high up, well out of my reach, on the mantelpiece. It had a black, thick, heavy fringe of Roman numerals round the edge. It gave the clock face an expression of intense wickedness which contrasted oddly with the innocent softness of its ticking.

There were a number of dark-greenish oil paintings

done by an amateur soldier-painter who was stationed with my father on Inch Combe in the Firth of Forth. They were pictures of stormy seas in the Firth and round the Bass Rock, wave-lashed islands and densely-leaved forests. In dark rosewood frames, these lent a sombre dignity to our front room. There was an enlarged coloured photograph of myself at the age of three in fancy dress— as Little Lord Fauntleroy—in a large oval gilt frame, looking angelic; and a photograph of my Uncle Jack at his wedding in Hamilton, Bermuda, with his pretty native bride, my Aunt Eulalie. There was a picture of a young lady in Renaissance costume: she had a sweet, fair face with a smiling mouth and mild blue eyes. In the dusky room, with the firelight playing on her face, her lips often seemed to move, as if she were trying to speak to me. But though I listened hard, with a mixture of dread and wonder, I could never quite catch what she was saying. A few years later, when I read *The Adventures of Huckleberry Finn*, I came across this passage which reminded me of the beautiful lady and deepened my great affection for Huck:

> Then away out in the woods I heard that kind of a sound that a ghost makes when it wants to tell about something that's on its mind and can't make itself understood, and so can't rest easy in its grave and has to go about that way every night grieving. . . .

Miraculous, funniest of books, and—oh, most remarkable Huck, the ideal friend, who understood things as I did! But that belongs to a later time.

The other picture at home which I studied in detail was a small reproduction, framed in *passe-partout*—why *was* it called that?—of " The Infant Samuel " by Sir Joshua

Reynolds, with the quotation from the Bible underneath:
" Speak, Lord, for Thy servant heareth."

The infant Samuel was dark-haired in the beer-coloured gloom of the reproduction, but I unhesitatingly identified myself with him. I knew his story well; it recalled the occasion when I, too, had woken up and heard a voice calling, rather improbably, I thought, " Jimmy! Jimmy! " I felt it should at least have been " James! James! "

Among our small library of books was a paper-backed, penny edition of Pope's *Essay on Man*, which was very dry: my mother called it " heavy," and my father told me what were the most famous lines: he had had to learn the whole thing at school, as well as " The quality of mercy is not strained " which both he and my mother could recite with dramatic vividness. There was an atlas, and every time I brought it out my mother would tell me how good at geography—and history—she had been at school, whereupon my father would begin to chant, in a mock-Methodist and highly irreverent manner:

> Tell me the old, old story,
> Tell me the old, old story!

We also had a volume of the works of Ella Wheeler Wilcox—I think it was *Poems of Passion*. It was bound in white, and the poems " gave me the willies "—I found them sinister and disturbing. I was much more fond of the large green volumes of my father's *Practical Woodworker*, with its countless fascinating illustrations of joists and joints and panellings and beadings and mouldings. I also read avidly each number of the *Journal of the Amalgamated Society of Woodworkers* which appeared each month, rejoicing to discover that the members called each other " brethren." Another delight was Arthur Mee's *Children's Encyclopædia*, from which I learnt all sorts of odd and interesting facts about every subject under the sun, and a few scraps of precocious French. It had very lurid illustrations: I remember in particular one in several startling shades of red which depicted a cross-section of an erupting volcano. *How to Make a Hot-air Balloon* was one of the intriguing articles " For young people to make and do." I never made one. It seemed too dangerous.

We also had a book of photographs of Edinburgh—there was a huge thistle and the outline of the Castle in gold on the cover—which included a reproduction of a painting called *The Murder of Rizzio*. My mother gave me an enthralling account of the life of Mary, Queen of Scots. I shall never forget the cluttered horror of that picture: the capes, the ruffs, the pointed shoes, the trunks and hose, the beards and mustachios, and the large number of swords and daggers. It haunted me with a very special insistence, because my mother had been to the scene of the crime.

These pictures and books formed the cultural background of my first five years. It was not too bad a start. Though I was soon to grow weary of such limited resources, I learnt to study them with intense concentration, and I was to find that ability to concentrate on one thing to the exclusion of everything else a valuable asset in the years to come.

*   *   *

It was not just the written word that interested me—I was as passionately interested in the spoken word as I was in music. Speech and music gave me the same sort of pleasure, an almost physical participation in what was being spoken or played, an acting-out within myself of all the notes, the sounds and the rhythms.

Besides the nursery rhymes I learned, I knew *Twinkle, Twinkle, Little Star* and a poem by Thomas Hardy called *The Colour*, which begins:

> What shall I bring you?
> Please, will white do best for your wearing,
> The long day through?
> White is for weddings, weddings, weddings,
> White is for weddings,
> And *that* won't do.

The next verses went through all the colours: blue for sailors, red for soldiers, green for mayings, until black was reached; the final verse was solemn and terrible, and as I recited it I felt doom hanging over me:

> What shall I bring you, then?
> Will *black* do best for your wearing,
> The long day through?
> Black is for mourning, mourning, mourning,
> Black is for mourning,
> —And *black* will *do*!

We had a second-hand gramophone with a green-and-gold fluted trumpet and an enormous, spluttering sound-box. I think I liked everything it played, from an ancient Edison Bell record of *Christ Church Bells*—which we played on Sunday mornings while I paddled my fingers in a bowl of dry Marrowfat Peas " put in to steep "— to the ballet music from *Faust* and *I'm Forever Blowing Bubbles*. We also had a very scratchy disc of songs and monologues by Sir Harry Lauder, whom I could imitate.

Home Comforts

The words of popular songs puzzled me as much as nursery rhymes did, and I used to take them just as seriously. The songs of my infancy still have power to move me to tears—*Ramona, The Sheik of Araby, Ever So Goosey, Goosey, Goosey, Goosey,* and the pathetic matey-ness of *I'm a Dreamer (Aren't We All?).*

I was very much concerned with the logic of verses like:

> How do you feel
> When you marry your ideel?
> Ever so goosey, goosey, goosey, goosey!
> Walking down the aisle,
> In a kind of daze,
> Do you get the wind-up when the *organ* plays? . . .

I felt unable to relate the state of mind displayed in that chorus with the idyllic rapture of *Ramona, Charmaine,* or:

> Your heart belongs to *me,*
> The sheik of Arabee!
> At night when you're asleep,
> Into your tent I'll creep. . . .

Something, I felt sure, must be wrong somewhere.

Street games, too, provided me with a spoken folk-poetry which I never grew tired of. Some of these—the ball-bouncing rhymes—I have mentioned already, but there were many others. There were the counting-out rhymes; I best remember:

> Ickle, ockle, black bockle,
> Fishes in the sea,
> If you want a pretty maid,
> Please choose me.

For this, the team stood in a line with right fist held out;
the counter hit the fists in turn with his own right fist,
starting with his own left fist; an unscrupulous counter
with a mathematical turn of mind could usually " rig "
the counting to suit his own ends.

There were some good skipping rhymes. On fine, long
summer evenings, the big girls in our street would bring
out a heavy length of rope that stretched nearly right
across the road. Two girls would take turns to swing it,
and the rest of them, in a long, giggling, clinging line,
would sing as they skipped:

> All in together, girls!
> Never mind the weather, girls!
> There's a lad around the corner
> Got his eye on Alice Horner.

My mother and I would sit at the front-room window
watching them. Though I longed to go out and join in,
I never did so: the big girls were too big and too rough
for me, and besides skipping was not supposed to be a
boy's game. (Though I didn't mind that: I used to play
with dolls and toy sweet-shops as well as with trains and
soldiers.) So I stayed inside with my mother, who would
be trying to read or sew, while the girls jumped and
bawled:

> Teddy-bear, teddy-bear,
> Touch the ground,
> Teddy-bear, teddy-bear,
> Turn around,
> Teddy-bear, teddy-bear,
> Walk upstairs,
> Teddy-bear, teddy-bear,
> Say your prayers,

140

Home Comforts

Teddy-bear, teddy-bear,
Turn down the light,
Teddy-bear, teddy-bear,
Say good night.

It was monotonously chanted, but if the game was not too disorderly, it was nice to watch the girls doing the actions in the rhyme as they skipped. They generally did the following one very smartly:

I am a Girl Guide dressed in blue,
These are the actions I must do:
Salute to the Captain,
Bow to the Queen,
And turn my back
To the boy in green.

I was obsessed by one particularly frightening rhyme:

In a dark, dark wood,
There's a dark, dark house,
In the dark, dark house,
There's a dark, dark room,
In the dark, dark room
There's a dark, dark cupboard,
In the dark, dark cupboard
There's a dark, dark box,
In the dark, dark box
There's a dark, dark ghost—(*accel*) G.H.O.S.T ghost!

Sung at nightfall, this was a very eerie little ballad.

When there were only two girls skipping in the big rope they used to sing:

Two little sausages
Frying in a pan,

One went pop!
And the other went bang!

Or:

Please Mrs. Bunny,
Is your bunny coming out,
With his hand in his pocket,
And his shirt hanging out.

That one I liked very much, because I thought the bunny
was like my mythical brother John.

And a girl skipping on her own would sing:

A house to let,
Apply within,
When I walk out,
Lizzie Brown walks in.

And on the last line, Lizzie Brown would have to "run
in " and take the other skipper's place. When they were
" all in together " again, they would sing, wriggling and
shaking as they skipped:

Jelly on a plate,
Jelly on a plate,
Wibble wobble wibble wobble,
Jelly on a plate.

Or:

Burglars in the house!
Burglars in the house!
Kick 'em out, kick 'em out!
Burglars in the house!

I can still hear those harsh, sweet children's voices as
they skipped and sang on the long summer evenings

across the cemetery end of Cockburn Street, where the housewives in their flowered pinafores sat on their crackets outside the wide-open front doors and the late twilight fell gradually over us all, while the first watery star winked over the river like the travelling spark at the end of the lamplighter's stick:

> Baby's on the floor,
> Baby's on the floor,
> Pickim up, pickim up,
> Baby's on the floor. . . .

12. *Excitements & Excursions*

On such fine summer evenings, if the next day was a Saturday or a Bank Holiday, we would cast a seaman's weather-eye at the heavens. If the sky was red, we would tell each other:

> Red sky at night
> Is the sailor's delight.

And we might plan to go on an excursion in the morning to Cleadon Hills or Marsden Bay or Cullercoats or even as far as Newcastle and Jesmond Dene. Next morning, we would be up early, and while my mother was preparing sandwiches and flasks of tea, father and I would be studying the sky. It was a bad sign if it was red this time:

> Red sky in the morning
> Is the sailor's warning!

But I don't think a red sky in the morning ever deterred us from setting out on one of our excursions.

When I was very small, Cleadon Hills was a popular place for picnics. The hills were very small ones, even to my infant eyes. I longed to see real mountains, with snow on their peaks and boiling lava and blazing ashes spouting from them, as I had seen in the *Children's Encyclopædia*, though I thought the photographs of the Alps in that *Child's Book of Wonderful Things* were very disappointing: the Alps, to my mind, weren't nearly high enough. I longed for such extremities of height that all human scales of comparison would appear even more ridiculous than the picture of a tiny Nelson's Column placed beside a page-filling Everest. Meanwhile, I had to make do with Cleadon Hills, which were pleasant enough in those days, before they became hedged about with semi-detached villas and bungalows. They were high, uneven, grassy acres, a good place for flying kites. To reach them, we had to pass the strange, forbidding gates of the Waterworks—I always thought of them as the Beast's palace in *Beauty and the Beast*—whose tall, Renaissance-type tower was a landmark, like Penshaw Monument, that humble, unfinished replica of the Parthenon, which we could see from Cleadon Hills. The Monument stands on Penshaw Hill, where one of the scenes from *The Lampton Worm* takes place:

> This feorful worm would often feed
> On caalves an' lambs an' sheep,
> An' swally little bairns alive
> When they laid doon te sleep.
> An' when he'd eaten aall he cud
> An' he had had he's fill,
> He craaled away an' lapped he's tail
> Ten times roond Pensher Hill.
>
> *Chorus:* ..
> Whisht! lads, haad yor gobs,
> An' Aa'll tell ye's aall an aaful story!

Whisht! lads, haad yor gobs,
An' Aa'll tell ye 'boot the *worm*.

There was an old mill, without any sails, on top of Cleadon Hills, and a white horse painted on a rock-face near White Horse Pond, where we could fish for tiddlers. There were flowering gorse bushes, and great beds of nettles, into one of which I once fell headlong. My face and hands and knees were covered with a burning rash which was miraculously soothed when my mother rubbed it with crushed dock leaves. The Hills were " all right," but rather unsatisfying.

Once we went to Newcastle, in a steam train that went through a tunnel between Tyne Dock and Jarrow, and over the dizzy heights of the High Level Bridge between Gateshead and " canny ould Newcassel." Then we went to Jesmond Dene, a well-known and overrated " beauty spot " on the outskirts of the city. I believe some of my exuberant cousins were there that day, playing football in a very dashing style, but I remember no more except the vast stretch of grass, crowded with trippers, where we ate our lunch, the cow-pat I put my hand in, and a shed where we sheltered from the rain.

Then there were Sunday school outings to Hexham and Warkworth, Corbridge and Wylam—enchanted places on the more rural, flower-sweet banks of the upper Tyne. We had to take our own mugs with us; we drank pints of scalding-hot, sweet, weak tea—the tea at Chapel " do's," my mother complained, was always like dishwater—ate bags of buns and ran races.

An excursion to Tynemouth and Cullercoats was much more adventurous, for we had to cross the river by ferryboat. There were two ferries. One was a very small boat

146

which we called the Ha'penny Dodger; the other was a rather grand affair, hung with gleaming white lifebelts. It had an upper deck where you could watch the captain at his wheel, and a saloon with upholstered seats. On sunny days, the water-reflected sunlight on the ceiling of the saloon was charming, and it made all the passengers look charming, too.

Right from the start, these ferry trips were exciting. It was thrilling to push through the stiff, noisy turnstile and run down the jetty to the landing-stage that rocked slightly, with an effect of mild hallucination, in the wash from passing ships. We would watch breathlessly as the great ferry-boat berthed alongside; the blue-guernseyed men vigorously hauled on the ropes that pulled her in and creaked ominously as seagulls round the shining bollards. Then—to go on board, to feel the freshening wind on the great river, to see the big ships come sailing by, escorted by fussy little tugs; a seagull perches on a rocking buoy, and then, after a blast on the siren, we feel the engines throb and hear the signals ring, and the boat is slowly turning, turning round! We see the landing stage with its late-comer, the houses of South Shields and the Tyne Dock Engineering Works gradually drifting away. How can people sit reading newspapers in the saloon? The smoky blue air is vibrant with hammering and the machine-gun clatter of riveting. A natty police launch dashes across our bows. Suddenly I find we are in midstream, and there's a grand gale blowing in from the sea. Then the prow, wearing the parted waters like a sea-dog's moustache, points towards the North Shields landing. We come slowly alongside. It is over. We disembark. Our knees shake a little as we set foot on Northumberland.

It was always a thrilling trip. But there was too much

to see; we just couldn't take it all in at one go: glance into the warm, oil-smelling engine-room, and the crossing was done before we knew where we were.

Late one stormy Saturday night, when my mother and father and I had been on a jaunt to Whitley Bay, we came to the ferry-landing at North Shields, and found—the last ferry had gone! It was a dark, wet, wild night: we could hear the sea thundering outside the harbour, and the river blackly rushing. My father went and found a flyboatman who agreed to take us across the river in his little rowing-boat. We went down a wet, cobbled bank that sloped away right into the river, and with great difficulty got into the capering boat. The boatman spat on his great hands, and shoved off. The little craft cavorted and plunged and rolled on the black water. The boatman stood at the stern and began rowing us across, using a single oar. Lights from ships glittered and light-ninged over the river: the water seemed very high, and we seemed very, very low. The wind grew stronger as we reached midstream, the waves roughened and the river seemed as vast as the ocean. I huddled in my mother's arms. The rain came pelting down, hissing across the racing water like whip-lashes. We had a small lantern that lit our faces with a ghastly glow and only seemed to make the darkness darker and the river vaster. The current started carrying us away towards the Black Rocks, so the boatman sat down and my father sat beside him, turning their backs to us in the bows, and they both rowed as hard as they could. We were still drifting. A launch passed perilously near, leaving a great backwash that made us dance and ship water. We were in danger, yet I felt a great happiness as well as alarm. It was something to do with the water: it was a friend, however violent. Worn out by the day's excitements, in the middle of the storm I fell asleep. When I opened my eyes, the lights of the home bank were beginning to come nearer: we were making headway at last. The rest was easy. The boatman stood up again in the stern and rowed us to the bank single-handed. When we disembarked, my father gave him ten shillings, which to us was an enormous amount in those days. But the boatman would only take five, as he said my father had done half the work. He got into his boat, and started rowing back to North Shields. Such is the spirit of the seamen of the Tyne: calm and intrepid. Cold and soaking yet, we hurried through the deserted town, back to Cockburn Street.

The other, northern bank of the river had a great fascination for me. " That side is *Northumberland*," I would say to myself, sitting on a bench on the pier and gazing across the river at Tynemouth Priory. It was a glamorous land, " ower the watter," where people spoke with a richer burr than they did in County Durham. It was a romantic land of moors and fells and castles and ballads, of lovely names—Otterburn, Warkworth, Alnmouth, Amble, Seaton Delaval, Bamburgh, Rothbury, Coquetdale, Wansbeck and Lindisfarne. . . .

> And he has burn'd the dales of Tyne,
> And part of Bambrough shire;
> And three good towers on Roxburgh fells,
> He left them all on fire. . . .

" Ower the watter," beyond the grim streets of North Shields and the Georgian elegancies of Tynemouth, lay Cullercoats, the little fishing village with the friendly, boat-laden beach and its quaint Victorian aquarium, where the floor was always wet with sea-water. Beyond Cullercoats was the coast road leading to Whitley Bay, that fabulous resort, hung with fish nets and fairy lamps, where the great ramshackle dingy *White City* amusement park blared and glared and glittered on the edges of the fog-banked Northern sea. My Uncle Bob once told me he would take me to " Whitley " and I thought he said " to Italy." I went home in great excitement that day. " He said he'd be taking me soon! " I told my incredulous mother, as I dragged out the atlas—it was not very far down the map! I waited weeks and weeks, hoping he would come one day and whisk me off to Italy. I never for a moment doubted his ability to do so, for he was a hero to me. He had been in the war, and, even better, he had been an actor on the stage of the South Shields Empire. Then one day my mother said to me: " He meant Whitley Bay, surely? " Then I realised, of course, it *had* been that, and my heart sank a little. Still, I thought, Whitley Bay is better than nothing. But somehow we never got there.

I do not forget the lesser excursions—the walks and tram and bus rides we had in our own canny town, when we went to leafy Westoe Village, that we entered by a narrow, echoing tunnel-passage between two houses, with white posts at each end which I vainly tried to leap-frog over. In days to come, I was to jump over them so easily! The village was near my Granny Kirkup's house. It was full of gracious houses, and sloping lawns and white railings and fine old trees. It was a quiet, almost rural place, cut off from the busy, noisy life of the town. I longed to live there. I used to go and gape through the wrought-iron gates of the big houses where the " nobs " lived—" the cynosure of local eyes." One of the largest, which I thought must be a palace, belonged to Sir James

Redhead, the shipbuilder on whose ships my father had often worked. I felt that it was right that it should belong to the Redheads, because it was built of bright-red brick.

Another pretty village, half-way to Sunderland, was Whitburn, in which there was a laburnum-hung, narrow, steep road called Sandy Lane.

In Cleadon village there was a fine pond for catching tiddlers, and trees and lawns and grey stone houses. Those villages still seemed very rustic, with their little war memorials enshrined in long grass and country flowers. They were so leafy, so grassy, so crowded with birds; and in the surrounding meadows the council houses and brick bungalows were only just beginning to creep up the lanes where blackberries and white and pink hawthorn and candytuft grew wild and free. I do not care to think of what the country of my early childhood looks like now, and I think I do not wish to see.

13. Some Festivals

"CARLING, PALM, Paste-Egg Day. . . ." Three weeks before Easter, I would hear my mother chant this litany of festive names. It was a familiar Tyneside mnemonic for the Sundays of Eastertide. The celebration of Carling Sunday—the fifth Sunday in Lent, or Passion Sunday—seemed to be falling into neglect in the nineteen-twenties; I certainly do not remember it being observed in the 'thirties.

At South Shields, on the Friday before Carling Sunday all the little grocer's shops would have a big dish of carls or carlings for sale: they were small, brownish-yellow, wrinkled peas which I believe were soaked in sea-water; some people fried them in margarine. They were always sold wet, and if you wanted to buy some it was best to take a bowl or a jug to carry them home in. They were sold at a penny a pint, and were very popular with "the kids," who used them as ammunition for their pea-shooters. Carling Sunday always marked the opening of the pea-shooting season, just as April Fool's Day heralded the beginning of the "hoop and guard" days, Whit Monday the top-and-whip, and 5th November the Jack-o'-Lantern.

I never liked carlings. I don't think any of us did, really, though children often like to eat odd and unpleasant things simply because they are told not to. I was told not to eat them, but I think I was disobedient to the extent of eating one or two, just to see what they tasted like. They were hard and insipid and were said to give you the " dye yer 'air "—diarrhœa. Nevertheless, children ate them in large quantities; it was a ritual, a tradition, and traditions are things which children do not willingly abandon. Children, the great conventionalists, are the most rigorous upholders of ritual.

I seem to remember being told that carlings were eaten at South Shields in memory of a Passion Sunday long, long ago, when, after a hard winter and weeks of terrible spring storms, the starving inhabitants of the town found a cargo of carlings cast up on the sands, and the whole hungry population went down to the seashore to gather them and to give thanks to the gods of the sea for this providential deep-sea manna. In my infancy, Passion Sunday always had an atmosphere of wild hilarity; in the Sunday school, carlings were aimed irreverently at the harassed teachers: the air would be thick with the flying pellets, and they would be rolling all over the school-room floor. Those Sundays still had some of the joyous abandon that must have infected all Shields folk on that first Carling Sunday long ago; it was, too, a ritual celebration of the first fine days after a long and disastrous winter and of the late coming of the northern spring.

Palm Sunday was an altogether gentler day, radiant with new sunshine that yellowed the pale grey fluff of the pussy-willow wands we carried to church and chapel. There we would practise the tragic Easter hymns that we would sing in the Market Place after the Good Friday march, when all the Sunday school children, in their best clothes, marched behind their church or chapel banner—

glorious, tasselled and fringed affairs of crimson or royal-blue silk adorned with highly-coloured Biblical scenes and scrolled scriptural texts—while parents and relations and friends lined the pavements of Fowler Street and King Street " to see the kiddars walk." Flower-sellers lined the route, selling bunches of primroses and dwarf daffodils. One or two of the famous colliery bands as well as the bands of the Seamen's Mission and the Salvation Army would lead us to the Market Place, where each Sunday school had its appointed area. The square was composed of seamen's pubs and ship's chandlers, and instrument-makers' shops, and we were always very conscious of the river that lay just beyond. Those were awe-inspiring occasions, when we stood round the old, pillared Town Hall—a great sea of children's faces broken by the taller figures of Sunday school teachers in charge, and by the great, wavering banners that flapped and crackled in the sea wind and flashed in the watery sun, while the sweet concert of thousands of children's voices rose in the seagull-sliced air of spring, singing:

> There is a green hill far away,
> Without a city wall,
> Where our dear Lord was crucified,
> Who died to save us all. . . .

I could understand only very imperfectly what those words meant, but I sensed completely their sad acceptance, and their tragedy: they sent cold shivers down my spine, and blurred my eyes with tears that were also caused by the keen, sunny wind. After the ceremony, there was a great fluttering of hymn sheets and the banners were hoisted into the air again like camels struggling to their feet. The bands would strike up a decorous but sprightly march, and while we awaited our turn to join the procession as it left the Market Place we would chatter quietly, pulling up slack-gartered socks and flexing rigid new gloves, staring at our companions' shop-raw clothes and at the stilled wheels of the colliery behind St. Hilda's soot-blackened railings. The mayor in his top hat and gold chain and the Town Clerk and aldermen and their prosperous wives, the cream of South Shields society, would lead the procession on its return to church and chapel, where we children were each given a free Jaffa orange. There was a feeling of community, reverence, sorrow, happiness and pomposity about these occasions.

Everyone was supposed to have something new to wear, even if it was only a new handkerchief; otherwise bad luck would dog him for the rest of the year. The little girls had new yellow straw bonnets trimmed with blue or pink flowers, and the little boys had new shoes and trousers and caps. I well remember the blisters I got on my feet after walking in new shoes on the Good Friday March, and the stiffness of the pockets in my new tweed trousers, where I would always find a bright new sixpence " for luck." We were all very proud of our stiff new clothes, which were always " hanselled " at Easter. We were sorry for the Roman Catholic children and the children of the large Arab community who were not able to take part in our March. I was not allowed to take part in it until I was four: I never found the March long or tiring. I generally walked beside Aunt Anna or her jolly little tailor uncle, Albert Earl, but I refused to let them hold my hands. I wanted to be independent, and besides, I had been well trained in walking by Isa.

The Sunday after Good Friday was " Paste-Egg Day,"

when we all had chocolate Easter eggs surmounted by fluffy little yellow chicks. I remember well the hard sharpness of their tiny orange beaks and claws, and the softness of the yellow fluff. My Uncle Bob delighted me by giving me two pretty china egg-cups with beribboned chocolate eggs in them, and my mother used to make coloured paste-eggs by boiling them in coffee or saffron or onion skins, and even, I believe, in Condy's Fluid. We always had a bowlful of brown and pink and red and yellow eggs on the table; some were wrapped in silver paper, others had little frilly collars round their middles and some were painted with clown faces.

On Easter Sunday morning we " jarped " our eggs. " Jarping " meant knocking your hard-boiled egg against someone else's, and the one whose shell cracked first was the loser. I don't remember rolling my Easter egg, but I believe many people did roll them on Cleadon Hills and Penshaw Hill, or in any steeply-inclined street: hoops were trundled at the same time. There were both iron and wooden hoops. The iron ones, which made a sweet singing sound as they slipped through the crook of the iron guard, were for boys only. They used to bounce alarmingly over cobbles and kerbs, and would fall with a very tuneful clatter on the flagstones. The wooden hoops were very dull; they were guided by a cane " guard," and only girls played with those. Easter was a curious festival in those days—half-pagan, half-Christian, half-sorrowful, half-happy—and it was lapped in the delicious aromas of chocolate wrappings and boiled eggs and oranges and new clothes. It could be wet and sunny, windy and fair, but it was always the time for new things—new caps and shoes, new friends, new loves, new aspirations.

My birthday, on 23rd April, was always associated

with Easter. I do not remember much about my early birthdays; but I know it was always impressed upon me that the day on which I was born was also Shakespeare's birthday and St. George's Day, and the anniversary of the Zeebrugge raid. It seemed too much to live up to. But there were little presents, and cakes for tea. The cakes were " shop cakes," which I in my childish ignorance and perversity considered immensely superior to those my mother made, and which we had every day.

Guy Fawkes Day did not mean very much to me until I had passed my fifth year, when I was nearly set on fire by a lighted "Shower of Silver" in my trousers pocket. I only remember that I stayed indoors, petrified with terror at the explosions of "Whizz-bangs" and "Thunder-flashes."

Remembrance Day, too, was a dumpish day. I never liked it, because of the guns at eleven o'clock from the battery at Tynemouth, the ships' sirens blowing more mournfully than ever, and the unearthly hush that fell on the streets during the two minutes' silence. I remember attending some sort of ceremony outside the Town Hall—not the old one in the Market Place, which I liked, but the newer one in Fowler Street—a black, forbidding building with a heavy statue of Queen Victoria outside. Nevertheless, the " new " Town Hall had certain delightful features. There was the statue of Hermes with winged heels standing on one toe on a glass dome, apparently ready to take off down Ogle Terrace and Beach Road and soar out over the sea. There was the great iron sailing-ship poised on a metal rod at the top of the hideous clock-tower. It looked so small from the ground; yet my father told me, to my great wonder, that it could hold seven people. One of my great ambitions was to climb up to that ship. Then there was the tremendous flight of stone steps in front of the entrance with its *art nouveau* stained-glass fanlight—those steps were wonderful for running up and down with Isa. There were enormous, fat-linked iron chains serving no sort of useful purpose—they just decoratively swagged the open spaces in front of the steps; it was grand to sit and swing on them. Finally, there were the statues of large, almost-naked ladies holding torch-style lanterns that lit up at night. Isa thought the statues were not nice, but I thought they were lovely, especially when it rained, and their dark, smooth flanks gleamed in the lamplight. A few years later, I was to learn a well-known Tyneside rhyme which goes:

I've seen many statues, great and small,
But there's none like those outside the Shields Town Hall!

I do hope they haven't been taken away, as the chains and Queen Victoria were. And I hope those open spaces in front of the Town Hall—fine for roller-skating on—will be preserved for future generations of " hard cases " —children who refuse to be awed by spurious grandeur.

Yes, Remembrance Day was a sad day. Mam was always sad, thinking of my Uncle Charlie, an " old sweat " who had been killed in the war. It generally rained, or there would be dense fog, and the fog-horn would add its lamentations to the ships' sirens and the thundering maroons. At school, too, it was a dreary day, for, as on Empire Day, we took part in the ceremony of " saluting the flag," which I detested: in any case, I couldn't do it properly, because no one ever explained to me what saluting was. Right from the start, I was one of the " awkward squad."

" What that child needs is to have all the nonsense

knocked out of him," I remember hearing a school inspector say about me. How awful that sounded! Always on " solemn " occasions, I felt more full of " nonsense " than at any other time: if I was told of an accident that had befallen some unfortunate person, I would rock with uncontrollable laughter until the tears came to my eyes; but at Sunday school bean feasts and weddings and children's parties, I would be overcome with melancholy. All through the boring solemnity of Remembrance Day, my heart was just a sodden penny poppy. I could not forget how my father had talked about the war—its bitterness, its drabness, its terrible partings. Sitting on his knee by the fire, I remember asking anxiously if there was going to be war again.

" No," he replied, " you'll never have to know what war is, because the Great War was the war to end all wars. There'll never be another."

I drew what comfort I could from that, but I still felt uneasy. If there had been one war, I didn't see why there couldn't be another.

" Did *everybody* have to fight, Daddy? " I asked.

" Yes, everybody."

" But weren't there *some* people who didn't have to fight? "

" Those who were very ill didn't fight. And the women didn't fight."

" Did the boys and girls fight? "

" No, they were too little."

" But everyone else did? "

" Yes. You had to. The only ones who didn't fight were the conchies." His voice held a touch of contemptuous respect.

" Who were they, Daddy? "

He told me, and I remember clearly that I did not reply. My thoughts were too deep for words, and we never had another conversation on that subject.

★　　　★　　　★

An annual event that filled me with a fearful joy was the ride on "The Figure of Eight." This took place always in summery weather. For a long time I refused, very sensibly, to be taken for a ride on the marvellously ramshackle old switchback contraption that shivered and creaked and clattered at the sea end of Ocean Road. The complicated, rickety struts and girders of its very Heath Robinson structure reminded me, though they were not nearly so regular, of the tartan criss-crossings of the Forth Bridge cantilevers, which I had admired so often in our Edinburgh picture book. The Figure of Eight was dirty-white in colour, and gazing up at it with infant eyes from the safety of the Mecca Tearooms, it seemed to prop up the blue vault of heaven and comb the passing clouds. Just to look at it gave me a horrible feeling of vertigo, and as I sat on my bentwood chair eating shop cake and watching the little coloured cars skim round the upper bends of the " 8 " and swoop and plunge among the sunlit maze of shuddering timber, I would feel my own head turning, and my heart sinking. But one day— it must have been getting on to my sixth birthday—I let my mother persuade me to go for a trip.

We got in a little blue car heavily decorated with shining brass and upholstered in deep red plush: we were the only ones in a car made to take six. As we waited to start, I tried to make myself comfortable on the seats, but they were so high and vast that I could only sit on the edge with my legs dangling and my hands tightly clutching the brass safety rail in front: I felt like a pea in a pod. The operator pulled a greasy lever and the little car, after a sudden jerk, slowly began to climb the noisy ratchet railway to the top. We passed huge, wobbling wheels, and lots of other very oily machinery. From far off, high in the splintered labyrinth, came the rumble of other cars and the wind-torn screeches of " flappers." The machinery was making a dreadful din. I peeped over the side of the car—all South Shields seemed to be gathered round the Wouldhave Memorial, watching our ascent. As we crawled higher and higher my spirits sank lower and lower. Below us, some seagulls were flying about among the struts: after that, I did not dare look over the edge of the car again. The wind was full of sharp points of sand and spray. I kept my eyes on the brass rail in front of the car, and on the sea horizon, that seemed to be getting higher and higher too. I shut my eyes. We were tilted back at an angle of forty-five degrees. Suddenly the racket stopped, we were tipped forward, and I felt myself whisked into space and falling with sickening speed. Just when I thought I could fall no farther, my feet flew up over my head and I began to fall upwards. We got to the top of a steep slope, and the waddling car began to circle one of the top bends of the " 8." The car went rocking and juddering along; there was a high wind blowing, the sun was blinding, and the whole contraption seemed to be limply swaying. Head first down we went again and whizzed dizzily up and round. When I opened my eyes again, we were cruising at breakneck speed through a flickering forest of creaking struts. Much of the wood was badly painted, and looked half-rotten, and I caught glimpses of several very rusty bolts working loosely in splintered beams. Another car full of screaming girls hurtled down above our heads on a track that swayed like a rope-bridge. A seagull flew right at us, then fell away in a long diagonal. A piece of loose wood fell clattering to the ground, but no one seemed to notice. There was a frantic jerk, then down we dived, and up again: this time the car didn't look as if it would get to the top, but somehow it managed to crawl to the next crest, where it stuck for several seconds. Then it suddenly hurled itself down again into the abyss of jittering, sunshot timbers where other cars were gaily dashing up and down and round about in the most unpredictable and preposterous fashion. They waltzed round curves above and below us, and shot down gradients that went right under our own track; then *we* found ourselves flying down under a tottering incline that another packed car was hesitantly cresting. Finally, a series of milder undulations brought us to the terminus, where I was sick outside the pay box. But after sucking a stick of mint rock with HAPPY SOUTH SHIELDS stamped all the way through it, I determined to have another trip—next year!

*   *   -

The most joyous festivals were Christmas and New Year. A week or two before Christmas, our little flat would be hung with coloured paper chains. Aunt Anna, who was very clever with her fingers, taught me to make some of these myself by plaiting strips of tissue paper. We made decorations with crêpe paper, too, but I always preferred the tissue paper—the colours, even the navy blue, were so bright and delicate.

In our house, the Christmas decorations were stored away from one year to the next. In addition to chains, we had paper decorations, most ingeniously made, that, when they were opened out, became balls and bells. We had one red ball, and one white one: I can still remember the springy feeling of the paper balls as I opened them out—how they rustled after being locked away for a whole year—and how difficult it was to fasten the little catch that kept them extended. We generally made two kissing-boughs, covering hoops with frilled paper and hanging coloured balls inside them. There were balloons to be blown up, too, and tied with thread while I held the twisted, bitter-tasting, rubbery-smelling neck between my teeth. However carefully and firmly we tied up the necks of our balloons, next morning there would always be one or two hanging limp and empty and wrinkled, looking very sad in the sharp morning snow-light.

We put sprigs of holly behind all the pictures and along the mantelpiece. We made artificial flowers—roses and chrysanthemums—and painted enormous poppy-heads with gold and scarlet lacquer: painted poppy-heads were very stylish in those days. On the walls we pinned our two Christmas friezes, printed on crêpe paper. One was bright red, and showed Father Christmas and his reindeer and his sledge in black silhouette. The other was blue-skied, with a big moon and snowy fir trees and dappled deer and a jovial, red-suited Santa Claus in a sledge piled high with toys and interesting-looking parcels. I thought it was the most beautiful picture in the world. It seemed to be singing out loud:

> Jingle bells, jingle bells,
> Jingle all the way. . . .

My mother would spend hours making puddings and cakes and mince pies. Icing the cake was a great event. Sometimes there would be snow, and frost-flowers on the window-panes in the morning, and long fringes of icicles hanging from the coalhouse roof and the rain-water tubs. I would sit on the table, close to the window, watching the falling snow. It was intensely interesting to watch the slowly-falling, twisting flakes as they came drifting down into the dark backyard. Up in the deep-yellow sky, the flakes looked black as soot, yet when they fell into our backyard, they were white as feathers. Snow was like the fire and the sea to me—a great natural beauty that nothing could spoil: the snow was as perfect as the flames in the grate and the long, rolling breakers on the sands, and I felt sorry when it melted and was trodden into black slush on our grim northern pavements.

I would often try to follow the course of one turning, shivering, drifting flake as it fell and fell, but could never be sure if my eyes had lost it and seized on another before it reached the ground. I loved the snow's absolute quietness. It was a stillness I knew well, and that I sympathised with. I would fasten pieces of cotton-wool to long lengths of white thread and hang them inside the white lace curtains, against the window-panes, like an arrested snowstorm in the house, and then I would gaze and gaze and gaze through the artificial snowflakes at the real snowflakes falling outside, falling so densely, so silently, so steadily, that a kind of hallucination would gradually come upon me, my eyes would stare and stare until they went out of focus, and I would slowly begin to feel that the veils of snow were no longer falling: they were still, and I was rising, and the window, and the table I sat on, and the whole heavy house were rising weightlessly with me. After the first shock of this optical illusion, I would often allow myself to drift into its smoothly-rising, unbroken reveries. But when I tried to explain my hallucinations to others, no one knew what I meant, and I myself laughed at my own seriousness when I said it was like going to heaven. Yet I kept to myself the conviction of the reality of that magical event. I knew it *had* happened to me. Everything became weightless: I was lifted out of myself, and the whole house became as insubstantial as the snowy air outside. It was all real enough to me, and if other people didn't know what I meant, I wasn't going to insist. . . . Then the reverie would be broken by great pads of old snow, sprinkled with soot, slipping and scumbling off the roof, and falling like dirty avalanches into the deep backyard.

We had a tiny, artificial Christmas tree that stood in a white-painted wooden base made to represent a tub. The branches of the tree were of stiff wire covered with green thread and paper pine needles; each branch had a very realistic tip of lighter green, with an orange berry on the end. When the Christmas tree was brought out and unwrapped from last year's newspapers, there was the delight of pulling the folded-up branches into place, bending each one slightly, so that the tip pointed upwards. Then we would hang it with bright baubles and tinsel and stars and shimmering " icicles," and at the very top we clipped a brilliant blue bird with a spunglass tail, like the Nailsea birds in my Granny Johnson's glass dome of birds and shells and flowers. There were holders for candles on the tree, too, and we put brightly-coloured candles in them. Unfortunately, as the tree was of paper, we could not light them, but I didn't mind—it was even more wonderful to imagine what the tree would look like if they were lit.

On Christmas Eve, I always hung both my stockings at the foot of my bed; I would fall into a deep sleep from which

I would waken to hear the carol-singers and the hand-bell ringers in the street. I remember hearing *While Shepherds Watched*, and thinking that the singers must be the shepherds themselves, and that the hand-bells were the voice of the angel. Their voices sounded queer in the snow, in the deep middle of the dark night. Yet it was a nice, happy sound, better by far than the hoarse call of the knocker-up or the muffled oaths of the scavengers. I felt there really were angels in the air at Christmastide.

Finding both stockings filled on Christmas morning was almost more than I could believe: it seemed odd to be getting so much at once, and for nothing, because I was led to believe that the things Santa brought were free. Somehow I could never quite swallow that. I felt obscurely that there was a conspiracy somewhere, but I tried not to think about it, and willingly played my part in the illusion. It was not difficult to do so, because in spite of my scepticism, I was sure that Santa Claus was a real person, and I went on believing in him much longer than most children do nowadays. So I would be up early on Christmas morning, sorting out the little packets in the stockings, and marvelling how every inch of them was packed with things. There would be a long box of dates—spelt on the cover " Dattes "—in the leg of one of the stockings: I loved the pretty picture on the lid, and the frilly white paper round the inside. In the leg of the other stocking there might be a box of candied fruits, with a small gilt trident to spear them with. There would be little dolls and motor cars and chocolate cigars and sugar mice and a little bag of gilt-papered chocolate sovereigns. There might be books of " Billy-Stampers " and little paper volumes of fairy tales. And there were tangerines and apples and nuts and hankies to fill in the empty corners.

Some Festivals

I was once given some handkerchiefs with stories on them: I hardly liked to blow my nose on my favourite literature, but it was always a delightful surprise to read *Ali Baba and the Forty Thieves* or *Bluebeard* on those linen squares, and I loved washing out *Goody Two-Shoes* under the tap.

After breakfast, I would run along to Granny Johnson's to show them all my treasures, and was always astonished to find that Father Christmas had called there, too, with presents for me.

" But how does he know I know *you*? " I would ask them all, and wonder at the laughter my question provoked.

" Wise bairn! " my Granny would say, her fine hand grasping a glass of stout. They gave me lovely presents: I can still remember a huge, brilliantly-painted humming-top, and a set of alphabet bricks that could be built up into a tower that it was great fun to knock down.

At lunch-time, Granny Kirkup and Aunt Anna would arrive for Christmas dinner, bearing still more presents from Father Christmas—a clockwork doll or a book, and once a Hornby train. In the afternoon and after tea I would dress up and dance and sing and recite for them, and then, as they talked round the fire and sipped their ginger wine, I would fall contentedly asleep on the hearth-rug, my treasures spread out all around me, and the decorations draped like the hangings of a fairy tent above my head. Our two little rooms looked bare when they were taken down.

One of my earliest unpleasant memories is connected with Christmas. I must have been only about two years old at the time, because I remember being carried in my mother's arms into a theatre. " Theatre " is really too noble a word for it: it was, I think, a large hall with a curtained platform at one end. The hall was near the sea, beside the blue-and-white lifeboat under its Moorish canopy, beside the Figure of Eight and the Mecca Tearooms and the tram terminus at the Wouldhave Memorial in Ocean Road. The matinée performance must have begun when we entered because we sat in pitch darkness near the back of the hall; I think the sudden darkness after the wave-lit brightness of Ocean Road may have contributed to my fright. It was a pantomime —*Jack in the Beanstalk*—that was offered to my startled gaze. I knew it was all perfectly horrible, yet I didn't know why. Then a line of chorus girls came on, in very brief red satin skirts and with huge floppy orange bows in their hair, and started kicking their legs in the air and shuffling and stamping their feet with hectic vigour. As they danced, they sang, with the vivacious, breathless flatness of third-rate hoofers. This was the crowning horror. I turned my head away and refused to look at the stage, and let out shriek after shriek of utter dismay and frightened fury. Nothing would quiet me. The girls went on and on, and so did I. Finally, my puzzled mother —" I was *mad* with you," she told me years later—carried me outside, still screaming as if all the chorus girls in hell were after me.

A few years later, I went to a pantomime at the Empire, and was completely won over when the foot-lights went up on the red plush curtain, and I saw the dancers' feet tapping in the gap between the floor of the stage and the gold-fringed curtain, while a dashing band cantered irresistibly through the breath-taking thrills of *The Post Horn Gallop*.

But in the North of England, New Year is an almost greater festival than Christmas. On the last evening of the old year, everyone sits up until after midnight " to see the New Year in." I was generally too sleepy to stay awake, and after a glass of ginger wine that made my throat tickle I would go to bed, to be wakened at midnight by bells and maroons and hooting sirens and laughter and shouting and singing in the streets. It was very important to have a good " first-foot ": the first person to enter the house after the old year had ended had to be a *dark* man carrying a lump of coal for luck. Then there would be kisses and laughter and wine and cigars and the singing of *Auld Lang Syne*, while the streets rang all night long with the shouts of first-footers calling out to each other:

" Happy New Yair, hinney! "

" Aye, and many of them! " the reply would come.

" May yer lum aalways reek! " my Granny Johnson would cry, with fine Scots relish.

It was always a great holiday, a fitting start to the year, and celebrated with the zest and gaiety and warm hospitality for which Tynesiders are famed all the world over.

*   *   *

These were the landmarks in our northern calendar, with August Bank Holiday as the summer festival. Whitsuntide and Race Week—when the Pitman's Derby was held on Newcastle Town Moor—were late spring and early summer celebrations; Blackberry Week was the October school break between summer and winter, when we went with our jugs and jam jars along the coal-dusted semi-country lanes to pick the stunted, half-ripe berries and gather the sea-coal washed on to the beaches by the first autumn storms.

But these were lesser dates in the Geordie calendar, in which the New Year was always the greatest.

14. *A Day by the Sea*

YES, THE sea was always there. We did not actually ignore it, or ever foolishly disregard the dreadful power that lay beneath a smiling summer calm. We were aware of it rather as a faintly-moving backcloth to our lives, as the inland city dweller is aware of the heavens, or the country housewife of the fields and hills. We never thought of " beauty," yet we knew it was beautiful as well as terrible. A long, rolling wave, sullenly progressing, swelling and tapering into blown spray, breaking reluctantly into white and toppling crests that slowly plunged on the thundering sand and churned the shuddering under-shingle was to me a perfect thing, beyond judgment, like fire or snowfall.

The whole sea was beyond human judgment. It obeyed its own inscrutable laws. It could make itself blue or green or brown or grey or black: it could be fierce or gentle as it pleased. Sometimes it would be far out in the bay, leaving wet acres of softly-smooth or hard-ribbed sand; sometimes it came too close for comfort, and exploded over the piers and the harbour walks, flinging the pounded spray high over the roof-tops of the coast-guards' cottages and the Majestic Ballroom. It was always the same, because it was always different. It

---

A Day by the Sea

shifted, and was shiftless. It rose and fell, and became no higher, and no lower. It was both deep and shallow, profound and obvious. It was all these things, yet none of them—a presence, yet a negation of presence that was not absence. It was tense and male; it was female and relaxed. It groaned and sang, howled and whispered, roared and muttered. It was never silent, yet it was silence itself, a deep silence that faintly hissed and mewed with the suspense of its own stillness. It was all, and nothing.

We used to forget it, spent days without thinking about it, months and years without seeing it, though it was only, as it were, in the next backyard, in the next street. And if we did happen to catch a glimpse of it at the turning of an unfamiliar lane, we looked away again and thought nothing of it.

But there were days in our brief northern summer when the sun blazed with unexpected savagery. The streets would be hot, airless, dirty. In the afternoons, front-room blinds, yellow and cracked, would be pulled down over all the sun-struck windows, as if there were a funeral in the street. The flagstones would be dusty and sandy, too hot to touch in their furnaces of brick. The shaded house would be full of dancing lights: reflected sun from windows over the way playing into the gloom of our kitchen; splintered, liquid rays from the unrefreshed dead-flower water in a cut-glass vase; children with pocket-mirrors—" bobby dazzlers," we called them— shining their darting, " impittent " beams on the back- yard wall and into the dim privacies of upper bedrooms; pools left in the road by the water-cart would sprinkle the ceiling with wet gutter and cobble reflections and flicker- ing puddle flashes made by drinking birds. The big girls going by in their summer dresses would send a white,

171

passing glare over the parched ceiling. Strange cats would lie in the cool of the washhouse, and mad, panting dogs would course down the middle of Cockburn Street with the hot sun glowing through the brilliant crimson of their lolling tongues. The dirt between the flagstones and the cobbles caked hard and dry, and cracked into tiny chasms. In the household grates, sooty-folded fans made of old newspaper leaned half-way up the chimney-back; the black-leaded grate would be cold and untarnished, the fire-irons, the brass fender and the candlesticks briefly chill to the fevered touch. Dullness, emptiness, dead heat. . . .

The lifelessness of the street would gradually bring itself to our consciousness; then we would jump up and say:

" They must have all gone to the sands."

" Yis, they must have done."

" Howway, we'll haddaway te the sands."

My mother would pack some sandwiches, and screw some dry tea and sugar into separate paper twists. Wrapping cups, spoons, a jug and the second-best teapot in a tattered traycloth, we would set off for the sands. I would be wearing sandshoes and carrying a spade and bucket, and perhaps a little yacht, that always capsized at the slightest breath of wind, to sail in the pools.

On our way to the beach, I would plead to be taken into the South Shields Museum and Art Gallery, where children could not be admitted " unless accompanied by adults." The Museum was housed upstairs in the Library building. I was impressed by the flight of stairs that divided half-way up into a double flight. There were fine mahogany bannisters, marvellous for slides. From the landing one could look down on the model sailing ship enshrined in its glass case in the entrance hall—an adored and almost sacred object. The walls of the staircase were hung with lots of big, dull, dark oil paintings in dingy gilt frames—drab seascapes of improbable, yeasty seas and foundering ships, or bland portraits of local worthies and benefactors. There was a large case of antique coins, some of them found in our own Roman Remains, between the door of the museum and the door of the art gallery—medallions of dark and light on squares of light and dark, all glazed over with glaring, twisty glass.

Even on a radiantly fine summer's day, the interior of the museum was like an unlighted aquarium, dark and cold, for it faced due north. When one's eyes had become accustomed to the dazzling gloom, one became aware of a large, dun-coloured, black-gummed lion gazing out of a glass case on the right inside the door. It stood still, stiff and cold, a single speck of white light from the windows refracted in its cold, glazed eye. There were other animals in the dimness of the ordered, glassy glades: a puma, I believe, and a leopard, a tiger, monkeys and a fox—all frozen into fixed, toy-like attitudes in this high, chill northern room, with the trams grinding and squealing outside, and bill-posters advertising *King Kong* over the Scala Picture House opposite.

There were grisly snakes, crinkly-scaled and beautifully marked, coiled in bottles or in glass-fronted boxes filled with rocks and artificial moss and ferns. There were stuffed birds—gannets, Arctic terns, cormorants, penguins, herons, owls, kingfishers, and a host of little brown and brightly-plumaged birds, all perched and crowded in suspended animation on a model bush, and all seeming to chirp and twitter soundlessly behind our bird-pecked reflections in the plate glass. Of all these dead things, the little birds were the liveliest. They filled me with a suffocating sadness, the melancholy one feels when looking at a photograph of an animated street scene taken long ago.

I did not like the art gallery: the pictures were not as bright and cheerful as the ones we had at home. There was nothing to equal our coloured print of a clipper in full sail on a choppy sea, called *Off Valparaiso*. But there were some good water colours of local scenes in Tynemouth and Cullercoats by a North Shields artist which I remember gave me pleasure because they were real, and represented scenes that I had visited myself. But I felt it was strange that anyone should want to paint old houses and boats and the local beaches and the sea, which after all was nothing very remarkable, was it?

The sea! Out of the building we would rush, taking deep breaths of the warm vinegar-and-salt-scented air. Over the road we would run, to be on the sunny side, where the Marine School and the long, forbidding front of Ocean Road Boys' School and the grey-brick boarding-houses soaked in the hot sun. In the darkness on the other side of the street the shop windows would be glittering palely, our reflections flickering over piles of sweets and blouses and bottles and the gold-rimmed china pyramids in the British and Oriental China Stores. In the dim shop doorways the swags of jokey postcards and beach-toys swung and rattled and flashed. Farther along, if I was lucky, my mother would buy me a ha'penny ice-cream cornet at the Italian ice-cream saloon, where you could buy elaborate ices for as much as sixpence; a bob—unbelievable luxury—for doubles.

The jigging tram wires came to an end, and now we could smell and hear the sea. But it was not just the sea we could hear: its soft, hazy rustlings and gentle summer lungeings would be covered by a shriller sound—the shouting and crying of thousands of children, the hysterical barking of scores of dogs, the laughter and screaming of innumerable family parties and chapel outings. If we arrived in the afternoon, the vast sands would already be swarming with people and plotted with deck-chairs, perambulators and long rows of lime-green tents. The pier divided the sands into two parts. Coming down Pier Approach there was a smaller beach on our left, stretching under the grassy Lawe towards the oil-tanks of the riverside and bounded by a smaller pier, beloved by fishermen, called " The Groyne." This beach was considered to be " low class." There were boulders covered with green slime, and the sand, strewn with broken bottles and fish-and-chip papers, looked filthy and uninviting. Crowds of poor, ragged children played there: here their normally barefoot condition was less distressing than in the streets—I had tried walking barefoot in the streets myself, and my feet had found it very painful and very cold. There would be bus-loads of rowdy trippers in hot, dusty, best-suited clumps drinking jugs of ale, eating saveloys and cream cakes with uproarious enjoyment. Though I do not think I was brought up to be a snob, I was perhaps unnaturally fastidious and sensitive to squalor. These feelings were shared by my mother and father, so we never went "on the low sands."

A little farther along the pier, turning to the right past the blockyard and the lookout headquarters of the South Shields Volunteer Life Brigade, at the beginning of the sand-strewn, cement-balustraded promenade " the big sands " came into view, broad and smooth and golden, stretching for over a mile to the grassy cliffs of the wreck-haunted Trow Rocks. The sands—we always called it

" the sands," never " the beach," which was a high-class word—were powdery-soft and rather grimy round the promenade approaches. But there was a long, iron-railed cement causeway that led straight to the rows of bathing-tents along the crest of the beach, and this made walking and pram-pushing easy for the first part of the way. But sometimes, looking for a less densely-crowded place to sit, we would have to plod wearily, dragging our hired deck-chairs—we could never afford the luxury of a tent—through the soft sand, our shoes in our hands, till we found a spot that was reasonably clean and quiet. But we could not go too far away from the little booths selling " Hot Water—A Penny a Pint," or from the little cafés where we might get a good cup of tea and be allowed to eat our own food with it.

Leaving my mother and father to settle their deck-chairs in the sand, I would run down to the sea—how far out it was sometimes!—to paddle, or " plodge " as we say on Tyneside. There would be hundreds of other small children at the water's edge. Sometimes little babies, upheld by a big girl's hand, would be staggering through the shallow wavelets or the warm sand-pools left by the retreating tide. If the tide was in, there might be heavy breakers that drove back to drier positions those foolish enough to have encamped too low down on the gently-sloping beach. Men and women in efficient-looking navy-blue bathing-costumes would trot smartly and seriously down the sands and dive headlong into the breakers, emerging far out, their purple faces spluttering and gasping as they swam and floated between the sickening rollers. I had no desire to emulate them. I refused to learn to swim, though I envied those bolder children who seemed so happy and fearless in the water. I was never able to entrust myself sufficiently to the water to be able to float even. Once I tried to swim, with a pair of borrowed " water-wings," but somehow I got them round my ankles instead of round my chest, and the experience of deep water in those circumstances was so disagreeable that I never ventured out again. My Uncle Bob scared me by saying that *he* learned to swim when he was a little boy by being taken out to sea in a rowing-boat and dropped overboard. For a long time I thought that this would one day happen to me, and I used to " go to the sands " in fear and trembling. My father consoled me when he told me that all the best sailors can't swim: then they know that if they are shipwrecked, and out of reach of help, the agony will not be prolonged.

Among the crowds of little children there would be large, fat ladies trudging along through the smaller waves, plodging with their flowered frocks tucked up into the elastic in the legs of their bloomers. The younger ones would scream and cling together if a particularly large wave invaded their skirts. I remember being terribly shocked and delighted once when I heard one of the old ladies exclaim to all and sundry:

" By! My knickers is *wringing* wet! And me back-side's bloody perished! "

Of course, I ran straight to my mother and told her what I had heard, saying the glorious words myself with the utmost relish. Sometimes these old ladies would be accompanied by a husband wearing a bowler hat or a cap, with his blue serge trousers rolled up to the knees, revealing dead-white, hairy legs and the cream ribbing of woolly combinations. Sea-water was supposed to be " good for the corns " and " good for the rheumatics " and " strengthening for the ankles." Some of the trippers would fill empty American Ice Cream Soda bottles with sea-water and take it home with them, "in case of emergencies," until next year's Shields trip came round. I was inclined to be sceptical, and regarded such pronouncements with suspicion. My own ankles, until I took up roller-skating, were very weak, and would "turn over" agonisingly if I stumbled on the smallest pebble. But plodging didn't seem to make them any stronger. I felt it was an old wives' tale, in the same category as the assertion that you could cure warts by tying black thread round them or that it was unlucky, as well as in execrably bad taste, to wear blue with green.

After plodging about on my own for a while, and making "pot-pies" with damp sand—discouragingly, puzzlingly shapeless before I learned not to make them with dry sand—my mother and father would come down to the water's edge and plodge with me. My father could make flat stones skip for incredible distances over the heaving water. I, too, tried to make them "stot," but I could never throw straight, or with sufficient force.

Then we would go back, dragging hanks of seaweed and a bucketful of shells and pebbles, and have our tea surrounded by happy, noisy family groups whose children I would look at with concealed admiration, but never speak to. If Isa were not there, I preferred playing on my own. While Mam took the jug and teapot to the "hot-water place," I would be told to sit quietly and brush all the sand off my hands. It was a tricky job, for the sea water made my hands soft and faintly sticky, and the damp sand filled the finger-nails and clung to the palms. I was not allowed to eat anything until my hands were perfectly clean. Sometimes I would go and dabble them

178

A Day by the Sea

in a little pool, and come back holding them up in front
of me to dry, letting them hang down like paws. But then
I would forget, and put them in the sand again. I was
an " awkward bairn."

Tea on the sands was a complicated and uncomfortable
business. One's bread kept falling into the sand. There
might be a vigorous game of cricket or " hot rice " going
on all around us, with badly-aimed balls falling on our
heads or into the hot-water jug. Naughty children would
throw sand, or run past us, churning up the loose sand so
that it fell in our laps and brown-sugared our tea. Or a
wild wet dog would dash up, impetuous and friendly,
jump on the flat mound of sand that we had built for a
table, and give himself a good shake all over the sandwiches. Worst of all, he might suddenly, ever so casually
lift a leg and pee on a corner of the tablecloth. And there
was nothing so irretrievable as a fresh-baked, buttered
scone dropped in the sand. But in spite of these vicissi-
tudes, a picnic on the crowded beach was an enjoyable
and exciting meal: the tea and the food tasted quite
different, and I would always have a roaring appetite.
On such occasions I was indeed " as happy as a sandboy."

There were so many things to do: I might go for a
ride on one of the small, brown, tired Shetland pit ponies,
" brought up out of the mines for a breather," and
incidentally to make a little extra money for their coal-
faced owners. The Salvation Army held prayer meetings,
with a band and bouncing hymns: I don't think they ever
went on the sands on Sundays. Certainly we would never
have dreamed of doing so, and I believe in those days
very few families did: even on the finest Sundays, the
beach would be almost deserted, and those who *did* spend

a Sunday on the beach were looked upon as very loose-living folk.

There was sometimes a Punch and Judy show, and one summer there were nigger minstrels with ukuleles and striped trousers. I rather fancy that Shields folk thought such things were out of place on *our* sands. Then there was a man who made wonderful sculptures in the damp sand: he could do mermaids and dolphins, and castles and sailing ships and battle-cruisers, with burnt-out match-sticks for guns. I used to watch him for hours, but he did not come to Shields very often. Once, after watching him for a long while as he made a low-relief sand-picture of the Shields Town Hall—copying it from a very grubby postcard—he suddenly turned to me and asked me what I would like him to make.

" What? For *me*? " I asked, incredulous.

He didn't reply, so I said quickly:

" Make me a Music Hall, like the Empire."

He gave me an " old-fashioned " look.

" You *would* have to ask for something difficult, wouldn't you? " he said gruffly. I didn't know whether he was angry or not. But he made me a theatre, with hanging curtains, and tiers of boxes at the sides. There were little shells for footlights—he asked me to go and collect them myself. And in the scooped-out pro-scenium there was a fairy castle and a bridge and trees made of seaweed—I got that for him, too—and a paper figure of myself sitting in one of the boxes, eating an ice-cream cornet. Then he made a little lake among the trees with a big, blue mussel-shell filled with sea-water. There were crowds of people gathered round, watching him. When he had finished it all by placing a tiny celluloid swan on the lake, he turned to me and said:

A Day by the Sea

" What do they call you, hinney? "

I told him, and he wrote underneath, in beautiful, curling script:

" This belongs to James Falconer Kirkup."

He made a fine flourish under my name, and added the date. I was speechless. He got up, picked up his capful of pennies and went away, and I never saw him again. Almost as soon as he had gone away, a big boy stamped his foot right in the middle of the stage. Broken-hearted, I sat beside the ruin, trying to make it right again. But it would not come right. It was drying, and crumbling away. My name, too, was crumbling away. But I sat there beside it until the sea came in, and watched the first wave wash it all away, leaving the sand smooth and empty, as if all that pleasure and wonder had never been.

But I knew I should never forget that man, and the happiness he gave me. He did not know it, but it was my sixth birthday.

15. *Time to be Going*

Lying in a boat of sand, I would watch the ships moving across the sea and disappearing over the evening horizon. The setting sun behind me would make my shadow tall and thin as I stood with straddled legs above my sandy craft and scooped the bulwarks higher against the advancing tide that foamed round the blunted bows. I would start baling with a little red bucket, but I would find the seat I had made growing wet, and my feet sinking into sucking sand. The waves would come nearer, until at last one of them would wash over the top of my boat, turning it into a muddy pool, and I would know it was time to be going. Tumbling out of my sunken craft, I would walk slowly back over the sea-steeped sands, watching always with intense curiosity how the wet sands blanched round my bare feet at every step: if I stopped for a moment, the waves came in and flowed coldly over my feet, then dragged back with an ominous sucking noise. It tickled the soles of my feet as it dragged the sand away, grain by grain.

I would look up at the high-and-dry beach, and see my mother collecting our things and waving to me. Most of the other people had gone long ago; we were among the last to leave, and the sands looked almost as empty as they did when we came early in the morning, before the noisy crowds came—the late and careless crowds, who had not known the vacant beauty of the beach at morning, and who came indifferently to crumple the laid-out velvet left by the night-long sea. I could not help thinking of them as interlopers.

When I reached my mother, I would suddenly feel exhausted, and I would sit trying to get the sand off my feet and legs. I can still remember the stinging towel-my mother used to dust the sticky sand off my legs, and how difficult it was to draw on my socks. Then we would set off home—a slow, heavy plod first, over the beach, while our shoes filled with still-warm sand. On the promenade, we would sit down and empty our shoes, then walk on home, into the dusky, red-fired town, towards the comfort and safety of our house in Cockburn Street.

I loved our town—the naphtha-flare-lit stalls in the old Market Place on Saturday nights, the shipyards and the moaning ships, the ferries, the sands, and all the decent, drab, dirty streets were all wonderful to me then. In later years I was to tire of its limitations, and move away. But I could never forget the love I had for it in my infancy, and which indeed I still have, though I have not seen it these ten years and more.

But most of all I loved my parents and my home in Cockburn Street. My mother and father are with me still, but we left that first home long ago. Soon after my sixth birthday I learned that we were to leave Cockburn Street: we were going to live in a bigger house, with three rooms and a scullery, a house belonging to my Granny Kirkup in Westoe, near my beloved village; in fact, I was told, it is in the same street—Ada Street—as your Granny's house.

I could not believe that we were leaving Cockburn Street for good: it seemed to hold the whole of my life. But soon I began to look forward to " the shifting," and to the new life that was about to begin.

.